NEW AND TRADITIONAL CUISINE

Heartland

FOOD SOCIETY
COOKBOOK

BARBARA GRUNES

COLE
GROUP

*I would like to dedicate this book to my husband, Jerry, who
brought me to the Midwest, and to a most wonderful editor, Annette Gooch.
Special thanks to Mindy Seigel and Dan Sarkowski.*

Please Note: Some recipes in this book contain raw or lightly cooked eggs.
Persons who are sensitive to these products should consult a healthcare or nutritional
professional before eating dishes containing these ingredients.

Publisher Brete C. Harrison
VP and Director of Operations Linda Hauck
VP Marketing and Business Development John A. Morris
Associate Publisher James Connolly
Director of Production Steve Lux
Production Assistant Dotti Hydue
Senior Editor Annette Gooch
Editorial Assistants Lynn Bell, Penny Hastings,
Linda Tronson, Jenni Thompson, Karen Forni

Copy Editor Sharon Silva
Design and Production Blue Design
Cover Photography Michael Lamotte

Distributed to the book trade by Publishers Group West

Printed and bound in Singapore

Published by Cole Group, Inc.
1330 N. Dutton Ave., Suite 103
PO Box 4089
Santa Rosa, CA 95402-4089
(800) 959-2717
(707) 526-2682
FAX (707) 526-2687

A B C D E F G H
– – – – – – – –
4 5 6 7 8 9 0 1

Library of Congress Catalog Card Number 93-31071

ISBN 1-56426-564-1

CONTENTS

INTRODUCTION

About the Heartland Food Society

Appreciation for and interest in virtually the entire gamut of American cuisine has burgeoned over the last several decades. Whereas in the sixties and seventies professional chefs and home cooks alike were infatuated with the culture and cuisine of foreign countries, beginning in the eighties they began to focus on culinary traditions closer to home. Food lovers who set out to explore their own culinary roots rediscovered the rich cultural heritage and enormous variety of the nation's regional cuisines.

In the spirit of that exploration, I joined with a small

group of Chicago writers, chefs, and restaurateurs to celebrate the varied and imaginative cuisine of America's Heartland. Concerned over the lack of interest by the food media in our region's foods and cuisine, we feared that the history and recipes of our beloved Midwest's significant culinary tradition might fade into obscurity unless we acted.

And act we did. Realizing that it would take something dramatic to bring the splendor of America's breadbasket to the nation's attention, we sent out dozens of invitations to food writers, chefs, restaurateurs, food growers, distributors, and gourmets, asking them to join us at the inaugural meeting of our newly formed organization—the Heartland Food Society.

Early on the morning of August 2, 1987, festive tables at the restaurant CHIC (the Cooking and Hospitality Institute of Chicago) were laden with Heartland delicacies. Slowly the temperature outside rose, nearing a record high, and with it rose our anxiety. Just before 10 a.m., when the first meeting ever of the Heartland Food Society was scheduled to start, we glanced nervously at each other and at the near-empty room, our faces mirroring our doubts about the outcome of the event. Then magically, as if out of the air, people suddenly emerged from everywhere, descending upon the room, filling every seat and all the available standing room.

The Heartland Food Society was born that day, its membership a potpourri of participants—from farmers to food distributors, caterers to chefs, gourmets to gardeners—people who shared a real love and appreciation for the vast, wonderful, rich food traditions of the Heartland. Our celebration of the Heartland had truly begun, and everyone who attended left the gathering that day with a sense of excitement and enthusiasm about both the heritage and the future of our unique culinary region.

The members of the Heartland Food Society all shared a strong appreciation of Heartland food and cooking and an earnest desire to promote them, to teach people both in the region and beyond its borders what makes up the Midwest table. That ambitious goal called for our getting out the word about the Heartland's expansive array of food products—meats, wild game, fish, cheeses, vegetables, fruits, nuts, and grains; its amazing variety of ethnic cuisines—German, Scandinavian, Italian, Polish, Mexican, Vietnamese, Greek; and its many different cooking styles—from the time-honored to the innovative.

In pursuit of our mission, we organized a series of celebrations and special events, showcasing the Heartland's exceptional cuisine: "A Taste of Michigan," a Heartland Food Society presentation by eight prominent chefs from Detroit and Ann Arbor, was held in Chicago. The first Heartland Fall Farmers Exposition Market, fueled by the produce and products of hundreds of Heartland farmers and featuring prominent midwestern chefs, opened at the Rosemont Pavilion, north of Chicago. And famous Heartland chefs traveled to New York's Macy's to demonstrate Heartland foods and cooking techniques.

Our efforts generated a bulging scrapbook of national newspaper and magazine articles and a shelf filled with new cookbooks and books on food, all of which helped to put our region's singular fare—and the Heartland Food Society itself—on the nation's culinary map.

I have written this book to honor both the Heartland's unique cuisine and the considerable accomplishments of the Heartland Food Society. This book originated in kitchens of the heart of the Heartland—of Illinois, Indiana, Iowa, Michigan, Wisconsin, and Ontario, Canada. The recipes are drawn from famed chefs and talented home cooks alike, from upscale urban neighborhoods and quiet back-country lanes. They are a mix of the modern and the traditional, of the simple and sophisticated, of the hearty and health conscious.

The Heartland Food Society Cookbook celebrates a national culinary treasure and invites readers to partake of a truly incomparable cuisine.

The following people have been instrumental to the success of the Heartland Food Society:

KAY ZUBOW, owner of Wild Game, Inc., of Chicago, who devoted hours of precious time to our cause and who has been a constant source of positive inspiration.

LINDA CALIFORE, "Ms. Hospitality," whose generosity, persistence, considerable capabilities, and skills have been fundamental to the initial and on-going success of the Heartland Food Society.

ELIZABETH (LIZ) CLARK, owner of Liz Clark's Restaurant and Cooking School in Keokuk, Iowa, one of the earliest and brightest stars of the Society. She returned from a summer in Russia the night before the inaugural meeting of the Society and, leaving her bags unpacked and mail unread, hopped a train to Chicago in time to attend the meeting. Her contributions were always welcome.

DAVID KORSLUND and ROBERT PARRAGA deserve special mention as integral forces in the planning, evolution, and success of the Heartland Food Society. They promoted and encouraged the efforts of the Society with great diligence.

CAROLYN COLLINS, an active Society member and founding director of Collins Caviar Company, Crystal Lake, Illinois, has summed up the role of the Heartland Food Society and the significance of Heartland cuisine:

"The Society brought us all together—producers, chefs, restaurateurs, writers. It was exciting and it worked....I think today there is no doubt whatsoever that America's culinary strength comes from its Heartland."

Heartland
FOOD SOCIETY
COOKBOOK

CHAPTER 1

The Roots
of Heartland
Cuisine

In geography, climate, people, and cooking, the Midwest is a region of contrasts. Teeming cities are separated by tens of thousands of acres of some of the world's richest farmland. Great limestone bluffs line vast rivers. Dense forests rise into clear blue skies. And each year all four seasons descend upon the landscape.

The earliest non-Indian immigrants brought with them the languages, cultures, and customs of their European origins. English, French, Dutch, Irish, Swedish,

Norwegian, and a host of ethnic place names quickly intermingled with the region's already established Indian names. Some communities, such as the Amish, Mennonite, Mormon and French Icarians, were based on isolationist religious principles; others blossomed purely because of their ethnic cohesion.

Today the culinary traditions of the Midwest continue to parallel those of the region's early ethnic enclaves. Specialty foods and cooking techniques have endured. The aromas of German sausages and breads, Nordic pastries, Irish and Czech stews, and Dutch preserves fill the Midwest air. Geography influences the table as well. The orchards and dairies of the northern states generate recipes based on fruits and cheeses; a variety of corn dishes prevail in the prairie states; the fish-filled waters and game-filled forests of Illinois, Wisconsin, and Michigan yield scores of popular main dishes; and ubiquitous home vegetable gardens provide healthful eating in every state.

NATIVE INGREDIENTS, NATIVE FARE

The mere mention of the Heartland conjures up images of rich, black soil; long, hot growing seasons; abundant rainfall; and millions of bushels of grain to feed and fatten hungry hogs and cattle. Put simply, five states—Illinois, Indiana, Iowa, Michigan, and Wisconsin—are the major food providers and processors for the nation.

This book celebrates not only the diversity of the Heartland's culinary heritage but also that of its harvest. The Midwest produces a myriad of fruits and vegetables, from garden-tended baby white asparagus to wild fiddlehead ferns. Black walnuts, cranberries, hazelnuts, horseradish, persimmons, and sour cherries are but a handful of the region's many products.

These fertile states are both the nation's Grain Belt and its top producer of beef, pork, flour, milk, cheese, and eggs. But these numbers do not mean the region relies only on mass production or turns out only conventional products. The flour sold by midwestern suppliers may well be stone-milled in the traditional way; the cheeses range from Brie and fine Wisconsin Parmesan to the wheels of exceptional blue shipped around the world from Maytag, Iowa.

In addition, small companies, some longstanding and some just beginning, contribute to an interesting mix in an ever-changing Heartland food panorama. Korean kimchee, a fiery pickled cabbage, is manufactured in Wisconsin; whitefish caviar is harvested in Illinois; and smoked buffalo sausages are made in Michigan. Game, both wild and farm-raised, from the entire five-state region is a growing export. Indiana alone provides much of the nation's duck supply, and Illinois is home to the country's largest mallard duck hatchery. Wisconsin is a leading national source of turkey and veal and also one of the nation's top sausage producers. Michigan vintners bottle fine wines that are experiencing an expanding national distribution.

What Heartland cooks do with this wealth of foodstuffs reflects the influences of the many ethnic groups who long ago put down roots here, as well as those who are settling in the area today. These vital culinary traditions have drawn upon the rich regional harvest to produce everything from German bratwurst and Scandinavian pastries to Italian breads and Belgian cookies, from home-spun casseroles to elegant terrines. And although Heartland cuisine continues to evolve, it will always be a uniquely regional fare.

THE HEARTLAND STATES: ILLINOIS

Industry and agriculture compete and combine to fill the economic coffers of Illinois, the Land of Lincoln. At the state's center is Chicago, "that toddling town," the Windy City, Hog Butcher to the World, City of the Big Shoulders. Many dishes now popular nationwide were introduced in Chicago kitchens: thick-crust deep-dish pizza, Chicken

Vesuvio, Shrimp de Jonghe, even Polish sausages, which were first sold by Chicago's immigrant street vendors.

The earliest French missionaries and trappers to the state discovered glacier-scraped flatland and frigid, snowy winters followed by scorching, sun-baked summers. Despite such extremes, Illinois is blessed with a long, productive growing season that makes it one of the country's largest agricultural producers. Alfalfa, oats, wheat, barley, and rye provide feed for livestock and flour for kitchens. Backyard gardens fill kitchens with fresh vegetables and fruits in the summer and fall and basements with preserves in the winter.

Corn on the cob is legendary here. Lillian Russell and Diamond Jim Brady were reputedly compulsive eaters of this delightful food, and Illinois home cooking features dozens of corn dishes, from fritters, puddings, and muffins to relishes and soups. When you open a can of pumpkin purée anywhere in the United States, it is likely Illinois pumpkin. The state is also the top national producer of horseradish, brought from Europe by the first Bavarian settlers.

Indeed, no discussion of Illinois is complete without mentioning the state's role as meat purveyor to the nation and Chicago as the center of the slaughtering and packing industry. Sausages of all varieties are a star attraction at county fairs, community festivals, and in German, Dutch, and Eastern European neighborhoods. Wild game and fish are also a treasured tradition of Illinois country cookery: deer, quail, and partridge during late fall and winter; catfish and bass in the summer and autumn.

Illinois also claims the title of Candy Capital of the United States. Leaf, Brach, Wrigley, Tootsie Roll, and Blummer's Chocolate are but a handful of the companies that have put the state on the candy map. But the Illinois sweet tooth doesn't stop there, with butter-sweet coffee cakes and Danishes crowding morning menus and breads and cakes fresh from neighborhood bakeries gracing dinner tables.

THE HEARTLAND STATES: INDIANA

Indiana can be described as two states surrounded by a single boundary. The northern stretch has the culture and physical characteristics of the Heartland, while southern Indiana more closely resembles the American South. The state is also divided along urban and rural lines, with heavily industrialized cities in the north and hundreds of small towns and villages in the more rustic south.

In 1800, the Indiana Territory came into being and pioneers of mainly English, Scotch-Irish, and German descent arrived soon after. They found prairies covered with wildflowers and tall grasses, crystal lakes, and forests thick with game. They soon conquered this pristine landscape with the torch and the plow, and Indiana became a checkerboard of farm fields.

Those farms now help to feed the nation. Indiana summers bring fields of tomatoes. Papayalike papaws are grown in the north, and the south is home to persimmon orchards. Although many Americans pick their mint in backyard herb gardens, the Hoosier State is one of the country's largest mint suppliers. And Indiana, birthplace of the baron of American popcorn, Orville Redenbacher, is responsible for a big part of the munching done by the nation's movie watchers.

Throughout the year, Indiana is host to a multitude of festivals and fairs. In the spring, there are celebrations extolling the virtues of the local maple syrup. Fish frys fill summer weekends. Autumn is a time for harvest food festivals. In the winter, ice skating and tobogganing compete with bread-baking contests.

THE HEARTLAND STATES: IOWA

The name is like the state—compact, stable, firm—and as rich with vowels as the land is with food. Iowa brings to mind red barns and blue silos, miles of gently rolling black soil punctuated by yellow tractors, vast seas of grain, rows of corn soldiers, carpets of beans and herds of mud-colored hogs. Lying just north and east of the center of the continental United States, the state ships its bounty in every direction to feed the nation.

The Hawkeye State's seasons are intense and predictable. Winters come on gradually and deceptively; by after Christmas, though, temperatures plummet and ice locks up even the mighty Mississippi and Missouri rivers. Spring is different—magnificent, fragile, and full of promise. Summer is the oven that cooks the food of Iowa, readying it for the fall harvest. Autumn is the glory season, when the earth, orchards, and gardens yield their riches.

Iowa cooking is seasonal and basic: candy-sweet corn on the cob, deep-fried catfish, juicy tomatoes, country hams, roasted wild turkeys, venison steak and sausage, and homemade breads. The richness of the cuisine is anchored by "plenty." Corn is legion, soybeans overflow the granaries, and beef cattle grow fat in thousands of feedlots. Iowa gardens brim with radishes, turnips, beans, tomatoes, cucumbers, squashes, broccoli, cabbage, beets, carrots, and turnips. Watermelon, pumpkin, and cantaloupe patches creep for acres; berries grow sweet and wild along fences, and nut trees cover the hillsides. Barley and oats fill bushels and bags; apples and cherries and peaches mature in abundance.

Iowa is the breadbasket, the cereal bowl. Its industries are farming and food; its people are farmers and food producers.

THE HEARTLAND STATES: MICHIGAN

For many people, sour cherries, tulips, breakfast cereals, and automobiles rolling off assembly lines are Michigan's icons. But the state's greatest asset is its landscape, a landscape especially rich in waterways. Of the five Great Lakes, four of them—Superior, Huron, Michigan, Erie—have Michigan shorelines. Thousands of smaller lakes and numerous rivers help justify the state's nickname of Water Wonderland.

Two years before the Pilgrims landed at Plymouth Rock, Frenchmen were already exploring the terrain. French trappers traced the lonely Michigan trails for decades before Dutch communities began springing up in the mid-1800s. In the early 1900s, Scandinavians settled the forested lake country, which reminded them of their homelands. The Irish and Cornish came, too. All the settlers carried their time-honored recipes with them.

What they found then and what Michigan residents and tourists still find today are lake trout, Coho salmon, smelt, whitefish, and pike. Michigan hunters pursue whitetailed deer, pheasant, quail, partridge, and duck. Woodlands provide a fertile environment for fiddlehead ferns, wild leeks, and chanterelle and morel mushrooms.

The southern half of Michigan's lower peninsula accounts for the majority of the state's vegetable, grain, and livestock production. Wheat is the main crop, but the productive soil along the eastern shore of Lake Michigan also yields large harvests of corn, beans, potatoes, soybeans, and sugar beets.

But perhaps Michigan's most marvelous vegetable is its asparagus. Its season, which is highly anticipated each year, runs from late April through mid-June. Row upon row of tender, young asparagus stalks, often sandwiched between cherry orchards, are handpicked, one spear at a time. At the Asparagus Festival in Shelby, the harvest is warmly greeted by both growers and enthusiasts who sample asparagus spoonbread, asparagus soup, asparagus salads—even asparagus cake.

Michigan is also home to some renowned food pioneers. Around 1830, Sylvester Graham, of graham cracker fame, became convinced that whole grains, especially wheat bran, were the salvation of the American diet. His views profoundly influenced Dr. John Kellogg, who founded the Western Health Reform Institute in Battle Creek and developed an easy-to-chew cereal made of tiny roasted grains. Kellogg and one of his patients, Charles Post, who invented Postum and later Grape-Nuts, forged a national cereal industry, and America's morning meals changed forever.

THE HEARTLAND STATES: WISCONSIN

Herds of Holsteins and Guernseys lazily grazing in lush green fields is the archetypal snapshot of Wisconsin, America's Dairyland. It is a state of rolling plains, thousands of lakes, high bluffs, and isolated buttes.

The first European settlers here, as elsewhere in the region, were French explorers, trappers, and missionaries. After the American Revolution, the English arrived, and then during the 1840s, Irish immigrants, fleeing the famine back home, landed in the southwest part of the state, where they worked the prosperous lead mines. At the end of the day, many miners burrowed into the hillsides for the night's sleep. They became known as the badgers, giving rise to Wisconsin's nickname, the Badger State.

Each ethnic group brought its own food traditions, many of which have been maintained. It is still possible to get an authentic Cornish meal in towns in the southwest, German food in Milwaukee, and Nordic pastries, redolent with cardamom, in the north woods. Soda bread, poultry with potato stuffing, and good beer are available in the state's numerous Irish pubs, and specialties such as pickled herring and pickled eggs can be enjoyed in the many small taverns.

Wisconsin's food reflects such strong ethnic traditions in part because intermarriage among its residents was infrequent. Entire towns became known as Slavic, German, or Scandinavian enclaves, and today many community food festivals celebrate these ethnic legacies.

But not all Wisconsin food is driven by strict ethnic traditions. Two million dairy cattle yield milk for tons of butter and cheese. The state is also among the nation's top producers of green peas, sweet corn, red cherries, carrots, and potatoes; and veal, pork, turkey, and duck are also important products.

Wild rice is native to Wisconsin's northern marshes. It was first harvested by the Chippewa and Menominee Indians, who bartered it for European-made knives. Today it is a delicacy prized throughout the country. Wisconsin is also the third largest maple syrup-producing state in the nation, and it takes pride in its delicious cranberry, buckwheat, and wildflower honeys. Hunters ferret out all manner of game, from deer and geese to ring-necked pheasants, and the many fish frys capitalize on the munificence of the region's countless lakes and rivers.

True to its north woods geography and the European heritage of its residents, Wisconsin offers a variety of stout and robust foods. Principal among them are the dozens of different kinds of sausages—*knockwurst*, *kielbasa*, *leberwurst*, *bratwurst*—first introduced by German and Polish settlers in the Milwaukee area and in dozens of villages across the state. These transplanted central Europeans are also responsible for making Wisconsin the top-ranked state in the country for the manufacture of sauerkraut and a significant producer of the nation's horseradish supply.

THE CANADIAN CORRIDOR

The foods and cooking of the Canadian corridor—the province of Ontario—are frequently compared to the culinary traditions of the Heartland across the border. The comparison goes beyond the kitchen, however, for the great north-south plug of the entire American continent shares the same climate, geography, and orchard and farming conventions, as well as the same Indian tribes and immigrants—English, French, Dutch, Irish, Chinese.

Ontario is a majestic lowland, with rich loamy soil that makes it Canada's leading agricultural province. Bushels of soybeans, corn, buckwheat, sugar beets, and other grains feed the province and much of the rest of the country. Oats and fodder corn fatten an abundance of beef and dairy cattle, hogs, and sheep. Cheeses are produced widely throughout eastern Ontario and fine Cheddars are common. Lakes, streams, and rivers make Ontario a freshwater-fish paradise, and wild game and fowl are frequently found on local tables.

Fruits flourish here, particularly apples. For decades every farm had its own small apple orchard, and today commercial orchards supply the province with apples and other fruits that go into an unending stream of pies, fritters, cobblers, and salads. The warm and sheltered Niagara peninsula, the most outstanding natural feature of the region, produces large quantities of grapes that help to make the area an important wine producer.

The strong influences of English and French settlers have flavored Ontario cooking for over two centuries. The venerable black-iron kettle, used on the indoor hearth and outdoor fire, contributed significantly to many of today's central Canadian soup and stew recipes. Cheese and cheese sauces and such pickled foods as mushrooms and plums are also popular fare in the fertile Canadian corridor, a land that embraces both the traditional and the contemporary.

CHAPTER 2

Made In Chicago

Center of commerce on the shores of a lake as big as a sea. Hub for harvests of all kinds, with its forest of legendary skyscrapers built atop marshes and ashes. Home to the third largest metropolitan population in the United States. "City of the big shoulders." "The city that works." Home to one of the world's best symphony orchestras and to brilliant ballet and opera companies. Rough-and-tumble sports town. That's Chicago in a nutshell.

Ethnic diversity, quick access to fresh foodstuffs, and talented chefs are just a few of the traits that combine to set Chicago's food apart from that of other cities. Once a settlement for Italians, Germans, Slavs, Poles, Czechs, and other Europeans, Chicago has more recently become a destination for Asian, Latin American, and other immigrants from all over the globe.

In the past, the Midwest may have been dismissed by some gourmets, but contemporary Chicago's vast array of sophisticated restaurant fare deserves recognition. It is still possible to eat a tasty, low-cost, five-course dinner at one of the city's many ethnic diners. Memorable examples of crosscultural cuisine can be sampled in the city's plethora of innovative eateries. And palates in search of haute cuisine can be appeased at any one of Chicago's numerous internationally acclaimed restaurants.

Culinary innovation is not new to Chicago cooks. Many dishes that have gained national popularity were first prepared in Chicago kitchens. Throughout the country, thick-crust deep-dish pizza is simply dubbed "Chicago-style." Chicken Vesuvio and Shrimp de Jonghe originated in Chicago restaurants, and Polish sausage was introduced by immigrant vendors in the city's outdoor marketplace. Turn-of-the-century dining in the city included the elegant teas and ladies' luncheons held at fine department stores and multicourse dinners in the homes of Chicago's elite.

OYSTERS BAKED ON SALT

SERVES 6

❋

DURING THE LATE 1800S, OYSTERS WERE OMNIPRESENT ON CHICAGO DINING TABLES. THEY WERE SUCH A STAPLE THAT THE GROCERS TEBBETS AND GARLAND SENT OUT WITH EVERY ORDER FOR MORE THAN TWO DOZEN A MAN WHOSE SOLE RESPONSIBILITY WAS OPENING THE BIVALVES. FOR OBVIOUS REASONS, TODAY'S GROCER HAS ABANDONED THE CUSTOM.

4 pounds rock salt

24 oysters, opened and top shell discarded

3 bacon slices, cut into 1/2-inch pieces

3 tablespoons butter or margarine

3 green onions, minced

1 large red or yellow bell pepper, seeded and chopped

3 tablespoons minced fresh parsley

1/2 teaspoon minced fresh basil

1/2 cup freshly grated Wisconsin Asiago or Parmesan cheese

Preheat oven to 425° F.

Arrange salt in 9-by-13-inch ovenproof casserole suitable to bring to table and large enough to hold all the oysters. Alternatively, use 6 individual dishes. Arrange opened oysters on salt.

In large heavy skillet fry bacon until crisp, then remove to paper towels to drain. In clean skillet over medium heat, melt butter. Add onions, bell pepper, parsley, and basil; stir and sauté until tender, about 6 minutes. Remove from heat. Crumble bacon and mix in.

Spread mixture over oysters and then sprinkle evenly with cheese. Place in oven and bake until oysters are cooked and cheese is lightly browned, about 10 minutes. Bring to table and serve immediately.

CHICAGO DEEP-DISH PIZZA

SERVES 8 AS APPETIZER, OR 6 AS MAIN COURSE

Pizza's Chicago debut during the early 1900s is shrouded in fiction and apocrypha. Suffice it to say that Chicagoans take their pizza seriously, eat an amazing amount of it, and are certain they live in the Pizza Capital of the World. Indeed, the city's deep-dish, thick-crusted, cheesy, tomato beauty is known all over the planet as Chicago pizza. Chicago's thin-crust and stuffed pies each have their local fans, too, of course.

Chicagoans traditionally serve three condiments for sprinkling on their beloved pizzas: hot pepper flakes, dried oregano, and freshly grated Parmesan cheese.

To make dough, in small bowl dissolve yeast and sugar in warm water. Let stand until bubbly, 5 to 10 minutes.

FOR DOUGH:

1 package active dry yeast

1 teaspoon sugar

1 cup warm (105° to 115° F) water

3/4 cup yellow cornmeal

2 cups all-purpose or bread flour

1/2 teaspoon salt

3 tablespoons extra virgin olive oil

FOR SAUCE:

3 tablespoons extra virgin olive oil

1 onion, chopped

3 cloves garlic, minced

1 can (28 oz) tomatoes, puréed, with juice

1 can (6 oz) tomato paste

1 tablespoon dried oregano

1 teaspoon each dried basil and sugar

1/2 teaspoon each fennel seed and salt

1/4 teaspoon pepper

Vegetable oil, for oiling pan

1 tablespoon yellow cornmeal, for preparing pan

In separate bowl, combine cornmeal, flour, salt, and 2 tablespoons of the oil. Transfer flour mixture to a food processor fitted with steel blade. Add yeast mix-

FOR TOPPING:

1 cup grated mozzarella cheese, or to taste

1/2 cup freshly grated Parmesan cheese

1/2 cup each red pepper flakes, dried oregano, and freshly grated Parmesan cheese, for serving

ture. Pulse processor about 5 times to combine ingredients. Process 30 seconds to knead dough. Dough should form a ball and be slightly tacky to the touch. If dough is sticky, add more flour and process 30 to 60 seconds longer.

Oil a bowl with remaining 1 tablespoon olive oil. Place dough in bowl and turn to oil top. Cover bowl loosely with aluminum foil and let rise in warm, draft-free area until doubled in volume, 40 to 60 minutes.

While dough is rising, make sauce. In saucepan over medium heat, warm olive oil. Add garlic and onion and sauté about 4 minutes. Mix in puréed tomatoes, tomato paste, oregano, basil, sugar, fennel seed, salt, and pepper. Reduce heat to low and simmer, 10 minutes, stirring occasionally. Remove from heat.

Preheat oven to 425° F.

Brush a baking pan or pizza pan 10 inches in diameter and 2 inches deep with oil. Sprinkle evenly with cornmeal. Punch down dough and press onto bottom and up sides of pan. Rim should be about 1 inch high.

Spread 1/2 cup of the mozzarella over crust. Spread 1 1/2 cups (or more, if desired) of the sauce over cheese. Sprinkle remaining mozzarella and Parmesan cheese over top of pizza.

Bake until crust browns well, about 20 minutes. Bring pizza to table in pan and cut into wedges (or in 2-inch squares if serving as an appetizer). Serve with hot-pepper flakes, dried oregano, and Parmesan cheese in small bowls alongside for diners to add as desired.

THE POLISH THAT STOOD THE TEST OF TIME

"Polish! Get your grilled hot Polish." That was a common chant of turn-of-the-century peddlers along Maxwell Street, the open-air market community just west of downtown Chicago. The marketplace was filled with people selling their wares from wooden stands, tables, pushcarts, and hole-in-the-wall shops. Crowds overflowed the sidewalk onto the sixty-foot-wide cobblestone street. Maxwell Street was never without people—some haggling, some buying—and the constant shrill rhythm of street hawkers. Food aromas were plentiful; by far the most unmistakable was the smell of onions grilling on sausage pushcarts.

It was here on Maxwell Street, in an area inhabited by recent immigrants, that the Polish sausage, a European favorite, became an American institution. For many it was what saved them during the Depression. A hot meal in a bun for a nickel was quite a bargain.

In 1890, Samuel Ladany and Emil Reich emigrated to the United States from what was then the Austro-Hungarian Monarchy. The prospect of selling sausage at the Columbian Exposition in 1893 drew them to Chicago and afforded them an opportunity to use the sausage-making skills they had learned in the old country. Their success at the fair led to the now-famed Vienna Sausage Manufacturing Company.

How should you make the original Maxwell Street Polish? Start with a Polish sausage and grill it until the casing turns a crispy charcoal-brown. Place it in a steamed poppy-seed bun, top it with mustard, and smother it with grilled onions. For a variation, add some chopped green bell peppers.

CHICAGO-STYLE HOT DOGS

SERVES 6

❋

EVERYBODY'S FAVORITE MEAL-ON-A-BUN HAS ITS ORIGINS IN THE MIDWEST. IT'S NO WONDER THAT THE HEARTLAND, WHICH GAVE US THE HOT DOG AT THE 1904 ST. LOUIS WORLD'S FAIR, STILL LIKES GRILLED FRANKS (THIS RECIPE FEATURES BOILED OR STEAMED HOT DOGS).

IN ANY CASE, THE ROLLS SHOULD ALWAYS BE STEAMED. A TRADITIONAL SIDE DISH FOR THIS MEAL IS CHEESE-TOPPED FRENCH FRIES.

6 pure beef hot dogs

6 poppy-seed hot dog rolls

1/2 cup yellow mustard

3/4 cup sweet pickle relish

1 cup chopped onion

2 large tomatoes, each cut into 6 wedges

12 pickled sport or Yellow Wax peppers (hot); pepperoncini or pickled banana peppers (mild)

1 cup drained sauerkraut

Celery salt, as desired

To boil hot dogs, bring large pot filled with water to just below boiling. Add hot dogs. When they pop up to the top of the water, they are done. This will take about 5 minutes.

To steam hot dogs, place on steamer rack over gently boiling water, cover, and steam until done, about 6 minutes.

To steam rolls, place on steamer rack, cover, and steam 45 to 60 seconds.

Place mustard, relish, onion, tomatoes, peppers, and sauerkraut in separate bowls. Set out shaker of celery salt. Place hot dogs and buns on individual plates. Let guests top their own dogs.

Italian Beef Sandwiches

SERVES 6

＊

Typical of many Chicagoans' no-frills, no-nonsense approach to eating are the city's hundreds of Italian beef sandwich stands. Likewise, hundreds of restaurants serve up this little bit of heaven. The details can differ, but the basics are universal.

First, the meat. Preferably a rump roast is used; the meat is sliced paper-thin. The gravy is actually juice and is never thickened. The bread, a top-quality Italian or French loaf, is sliced, although not all the way through. The meat and "gravy" are piled on the bread and topped with sweet peppers (or hot peppers or both!) Sounds simple, but the combination of the moist, hot beef with the bread and peppers is complex and satisfying. Add a beer or a Coke and you are pretty near heaven.

FOR ROAST BEEF:

1 teaspoon dried oregano

1 teaspoon dried rosemary

1/2 teaspoon pepper

1/2 teaspoon garlic powder

1 rump roast or sirloin tip roast (2 1/2 lb)

2 beef bouillon cubes

1 1/2 cups boiling water

To roast beef preheat oven to 425° F.

In a small bowl stir together oregano, rosemary, pepper, and garlic. Rub mixture over all surfaces of roast. Put roast on rack in shallow roasting pan. Dissolve beef cubes in water and pour into bottom of pan. Roast meat until very rare, 1 hour and 15 minutes or until a thermometer registers 125° F.

Remove roast and set aside on carving board. Remove fat from pan juices and use juices as part of beef stock for preparing sandwiches. When roast has cooled enough to carve easily, cut enough of roast into paper-thin slices to measure 1 1/2 pounds; save remaining roast for another use.

To make sandwiches, in deep saucepan over medium heat, stir together stock, water, tomato paste, barbecue sauce, oregano, red-pepper flakes, bay leaves, garlic, and ground pepper. Bring to boil, reduce heat to low, cover, and simmer 10 minutes. Stir in bell pepper strips and continue cooking 15 minutes longer.

Split rolls lengthwise three-quarters of the way through. Flatten, dip into the hot sauce, and place cut side up on individual plates.

Mound rolls with beef slices and bell peppers. Serve hot.

FOR SANDWICHES:

2 cups beef stock, including pan juices

1 cup water

1/4 cup tomato paste

2 tablespoons bottled barbecue sauce

1/2 teaspoon dried oregano

1/8 to 1/4 teaspoon red-pepper flakes, or to taste

3 small bay leaves

3 cloves garlic, minced

1/4 teaspoon freshly ground pepper

2 green bell peppers, seeded and thinly sliced lengthwise

2 red bell peppers, seeded and thinly sliced lengthwise

6 small loaves Italian bread

CHUTNEY PORK ROAST

SERVES 6 TO 8

❈

THIS SOPHISTICATED DISH IS FROM THE COOKING AND HOSPITALITY INSTITUTE OF CHICAGO (CHIC), ONE OF THE MIDWEST'S PREMIER TRAINING GROUNDS FOR ASPIRING CHEFS. FOUNDED IN 1983, THE INSTITUTE OFFERS CERTIFICATE PROGRAMS IN PROFESSIONAL COOKING, BAKING, PASTRY, AND RESTAURANT MANAGEMENT. THE INSTITUTE ALSO OPERATES AN EXCELLENT RESTAURANT RUN BY ITS STUDENTS. THE HEARTLAND FOOD SOCIETY WAS ABLE TO HOLD ITS INAUGURAL MEETING AT THE INSTITUTE, THANKS TO AN INVITATION FROM LINDA CALIFORE, PRESIDENT OF CHIC.

1 pork loin roast with bone, (about 5 lbs)
3/4 cup Italian sausage, removed from casings
2 cloves garlic, minced
1/2 pound onions, minced
1 celery stalk, minced
1 apple, peeled, cored, and diced
1/2 cup chutney
1 pound day-old cornbread, crumbled into large pieces (see page 81)
2 tablespoons chopped fresh parsley
1 tablespoon chopped fresh sage
1 teaspoon chopped fresh rosemary
1/4 teaspoon marjoram
1/4 cup apple juice
1/2 cup chicken stock
2 eggs, lightly beaten
Salt, cayenne pepper, and black pepper, to taste

Preheat oven to 325° F.

Ask your butcher to bone and butterfly pork loin roast to measure about 12 inches by 8 inches. Leave on 1/4 inch of surface fat.

In a skillet over medium-high heat, crumble sausage and cook until browned. Remove with slotted spoon and cool. Reserve drippings. In same skillet heat 1/4 cup reserved drippings. Add garlic, onion, and celery and sauté over medium heat until tender, about 5 minutes. Add apple and cook, stirring, 2 minutes. Stir in chutney until well mixed. Remove from heat.

Place cornbread in large bowl. Add sausage, sautéed mixture, herbs, apple juice, chicken stock, and eggs. Mix gently but thoroughly. Test fry a bit of stuffing and taste for seasoning; adjust if necessary.

Lay butterflied pork flat, fat side down. Season with salt and pepper. Mound stuffing lengthwise down the middle. Fold meat over the stuffing and tie securely with kitchen string.

FOR GLAZE:

1/2 cup firmly packed brown sugar

1 tablespoon each whole-grain mustard, honey, and dry white wine

2 teaspoons minced garlic

2 tablespoons minced lemongrass

pinch ground cloves

FOR SAUCE:

2 tablespoons butter, divided

1 onion, minced

2 cloves garlic, minced

1 tablespoon dry mustard

2 cups dry white wine

2 cups demi-glace or reduced brown stock (available at gourmet food shops)

1/3 cup good-quality bottled chutney

1 teaspoon Dijon-style mustard

1 tablespoon fresh lemon juice

Salt and freshly ground pepper, to taste

Place in roasting pan and slip into oven.

Meanwhile, make glaze. In mixing bowl, combine all ingredients and toss together until well mixed.

After 1 hour of roasting, remove pork from oven. Coat top with glaze. Return to oven and cook, basting occasionally, 30 to 45 minutes longer, or until thermometer registers 160° F.

While pork is finishing cooking, make sauce. In skillet over medium heat, melt half the butter. Add onion and garlic and sauté until tender, about 5 minutes. Add dry mustard and white wine and reduce over high heat by 1/2 to 2/3 cup. Add demi-glace and chutney and simmer, stirring occasionally until sauce consistency is achieved, about 20 minutes. Whisk in Dijon mustard, remaining butter, and lemon juice. Season with salt and pepper. You should have about 2 cups. Keep warm.

Remove roast from oven. Cover with foil to keep warm and let stand 20 minutes. Cut into 1/4-inch-thick slices. Serve with sauce.

SHRIMP DE JONGHE

SERVES 6

＊

AT THE TIME OF THE COLUMBIAN EXHIBITION IN 1893, AN ELEGANT FRENCH RESTAURANT, DE JONGHE'S, OPENED ITS DOORS IN DOWNTOWN CHICAGO AND BEGAN SERVING THE HAUTE CUISINE FOR WHICH IT BECAME FAMOUS. A FAMILY ENTERPRISE RUN BY FIVE BROTHERS AND SISTERS AND THEIR MOTHER, THE RESTAURANT BECAME LEGENDARY FOR ITS SHRIMP DE JONGHE, A DELECTABLE MIXTURE OF SHRIMP, BREAD CRUMBS, AND GARLIC BUTTER.

- *4 tablespoons (1/2 stick) butter or margarine*
- *3 tablespoons chopped onion*
- *3 large cloves garlic, minced*
- *1/2 cup dry sherry or sauterne*
- *1/2 teaspoon salt*
- *1/8 teaspoon white pepper*
- *4 slices day-old white bread, crusts trimmed, torn into quarters*
- *1/2 teaspoon paprika*
- *1/4 cup trimmed fresh parsley*
- *1 1/2 pounds extra-large shrimp (about 36), peeled and deveined*

Preheat oven to 350° F.

In large skillet over medium heat, melt 3 tablespoons of the butter. Add onion and sauté 2 minutes. Add garlic and continue to sauté 2 minutes longer. Stir in sherry, salt, and pepper. Remove from heat.

In food processor fitted with steel blade, combine bread, paprika, and parsley. Process to form crumbs.

Grease 6 individual oven-proof ramekins with remaining 1 tablespoon butter. Divide shrimp evenly among ramekins. Top evenly with crumb mixture and then onion mixture.

Bake until crumbs brown slightly and sauce is bubbly, 12 to 15 minutes. Bring to table piping hot.

CHICKEN VESUVIO

SERVES 6 TO 8

✳

THE ORIGIN OF CHICKEN VESUVIO IS SHROUDED IN MYSTERY. WAS THIS RECIPE INVENTED ON AN ATLANTIC CRUISE SHIP? WAS IT CREATED IN A FAMILY-RUN ITALIAN RESTAURANT? WAS IT BROUGHT TO CHICAGO BY A CHEF WHO HAD TRAVELED IN ITALY? WHATEVER ITS BEGINNINGS, CHICKEN VESUVIO HAS BEEN SERVED IN CHICAGO RESTAURANTS FOR DECADES. HERE IS AN ENTICING VERSION FOR SERVING AT HOME.

1 cup flour

1 tablespoon dried basil

1/2 teaspoon each dried rosemary and salt

1/2 teaspoon freshly ground pepper

2 chickens (about 2 lb each)

4 large potatoes, each peeled and sliced lengthwise into 6 wedges

1/2 cup extra virgin olive oil

4 cloves garlic, minced

1/2 cup minced fresh parsley

In a bowl, stir together flour, basil, rosemary, salt, and 1/4 teaspoon of the pepper. Transfer mixture to sheet of aluminum foil.

Cut each chicken into 8 serving pieces and trim away any fat. Pat chicken pieces dry with paper towels. Roll each piece in flour mixture; tap off excess flour.

In large heavy skillet over medium heat warm 1/4 cup of the oil. Working in batches, arrange chicken pieces, skin side down, in pan and fry 4 minutes. Turn chicken twice more, each time after frying 4 minutes. Drain on paper towels.

Add remaining 1/4 cup oil to skillet and place over medium-high heat. Pat potato pieces dry with paper towels and add to oil. Cook, turning every 3 minutes, until golden brown, until done, about 9 minutes in all. Remove from heat.

Preheat oven to 375° F. Arrange chicken pieces in single layer in large baking pan. Top with potatoes and any drippings scraped from skillet. Sprinkle garlic and parsley over potatoes and chicken.

Bake until potatoes are fork tender and chicken joints move easily, 18 to 20 minutes, or check for doneness by pricking with a fork; juices should run clear.

To serve, mound chicken and potatoes on a heated platter in a cone shape (to resemble Mount Vesuvio). Drizzle with pan juices and serve immediately.

Note: For extra crispiness, finish chicken by placing it in a preheated broiler 6 inches from the heat for 3 minutes.

ROASTED VEGETABLE AND CHICKEN HASH

MAKES 6 SERVINGS

✳

FOR HALF A CENTURY, CHICAGO'S PUMP ROOM HAS BEEN HOME TO LOCAL POWER BROKERS AND VISITING CELEBRITIES. ALTHOUGH THE RESTAURANT'S WAITERS NO LONGER SPORT TURBANS OR SERVE SHISH KABOB ON FLAMING SWORDS, MANY PUMP ROOM TRADITIONS, SUCH AS CHICKEN HASH, HAVE SURVIVED THE DECADES. THIS 90'S VERSION OF AN OLD-FASHIONED HEARTLAND FAVORITE IS FROM THE PRIVATE RECIPE FILES OF RUSSELL BRY, EXECUTIVE CHEF FOR LETTUCE ENTERTAIN YOU, A RESTAURANT GROUP. SERVE THE HASH WITH YOUR FAVORITE TOMATO SAUCE (SEE PAGE 179).

1 roasting chicken (3 lb)
3 tablespoons extra virgin olive oil
1 cup each diced red onion and diced fresh mushrooms
1/2 cup each diced red bell pepper, yellow pepper,
    fresh poblano chile, celery, and carrot
3 diced plum tomatoes
1 1/2 cups diced parboiled potatoes
2 teaspoons chopped fresh rosemary
1 teaspoon chopped fresh thyme
2 teaspoons kosher salt
3/4 teaspoon freshly ground pepper
2 cups fine dried bread crumbs
Olive oil, as desired, for pan frying
Chopped fresh basil, as desired for garnish

Roast chicken according to your favorite recipe or preheat oven to 400° F, place bird breast side up on rack, and roast until juices run clear when a skewer is inserted into thickest part of leg, about 1 hour. Let chicken cool, then skin and bone. Cut chicken into medium-sized pieces and place in large bowl. Save pan drippings to use later.

Preheat oven to 500° F. Heat large ovenproof sauté pan until very hot. Add olive oil, all diced vegetables, rosemary, and thyme. Cook over high heat, stirring, until vegetables begin to brown. Place pan in oven and roast 15 minutes.

Add vegetables to diced chicken and toss to mix. Season with kosher salt, pepper, and reserved pan drippings. For a crispier, denser hash, add 1 egg to hash mixture. Mix well and let cool. Reduce oven temperature to 425° F.

Form chicken mixture into 6 equal patties. Sprinkle patties on both sides with bread crumbs. In skillet over medium-high heat, warm oil. Add patties and pan fry, turning once, until golden brown on each side. Transfer pan to oven and bake 10 to 12 minutes.

Serve with tomato sauce and fresh chopped basil, if desired.

SAINT PADDY'S CLASSIC
CORNED-BEEF DINNER

MAKES 6 TO 8 SERVINGS

❋

EVERYONE IS IRISH ON ST. PATRICK'S DAY IN CHICAGO. THE CHICAGO RIVER TURNS GREEN (WITH THE AID OF NONTOXIC DYE) AND THE PARADE BRINGS OUT THOUSANDS OF WELL WISH-ERS. THE LUCKIEST REVELERS RETURN HOME TO FEAST ON CLASSIC CORNED BEEF, CAB-BAGE, AND ROOT VEGETABLES, TOPPED WITH A ZESTY SAUCE OF HORSERADISH AND CREAM.

5 to 6 pounds corned-beef brisket

8 to 12 small beets, tops removed

8 to 12 small boiling potatoes, peeled

8 to 12 small boiling onions, peeled

8 to 12 carrots, scraped

6 small turnips, peeled

1 head green cabbage, cored and quartered

Mustard, for accompaniment

FOR HORSERADISH SAUCE:

1 cup chilled whipping cream

4 to 5 tablespoons prepared horseradish

3 tablespoons cider vinegar

Salt and freshly ground pepper, to taste

Rinse corned-beef under running water and place in a large, deep pot. Cover with cold water and bring just to a boil over high heat; skim off any scum that rises to the surface. Reduce heat to low, partially cover pot, and let simmer gently for 3 hours. (At this point meat can remain in the hot cooking liquid for another hour or two if you wish to delay serving. Bring back to a simmer before continuing with the vegetables.)

About an hour or so before you wish to serve, place beets in a medium saucepan, cover with water, and boil until tender when pierced (30 to 40 minutes). Drain; peel when cool enough to handle. Return peeled beets to saucepan, add a few ladlefuls of the corned-beef broth, and keep warm over low heat.

While beets are boiling, drop potatoes into simmering corned-beef pot and cook for 10 minutes. Drop in onions, carrots, and turnips, and simmer until vegetables are quite tender when pierced (about 30 minutes more). Add cabbage wedges and simmer exactly 3 minutes.

Remove meat from pot, slice thinly, and arrange on a large warm platter. Surround meat with vegetables from pot. Drain beets and place in another serving bowl. Serve with mustard and Horseradish Sauce.

Horseradish Sauce: Whip cream until it stands in stiff peaks. Fold in horseradish and vinegar, and season with salt and pepper.

ELI'S PUMPKIN CHEESECAKE

SERVES 10-12

✳

ELI'S CHEESECAKE WAS ORIGINALLY CREATED BY CHICAGO RESTAURATEUR ELI SCHULMAN FOR HIS CELEBRATED EATERY, ELI'S, THE PLACE FOR STEAK. IN THE PAST FEW YEARS, THE CHEESE-CAKE KNOWN AS ELI'S CHICAGO'S FINEST HAS GROWN FROM A WELL-KEPT SECRET TO AN INTER-NATIONALLY KNOWN DESSERT, AVAILABLE IN RESTAURANTS, GOURMET FOOD STORES, AND DEPARTMENT STORES IN 48 STATES, CANADA, PUERTO RICO, AND JAPAN. USE YOUR FAVORITE GRAHAM CRACKER CRUST FOR THIS CHEESECAKE OR TRY THE EASY-TO-MAKE VERSION INCLUDED HERE.

FOR GRAHAM CRACKER CRUMB CRUST:

Butter, for greasing pan

2 cups fine graham cracker crumbs

2 tablespoons granulated sugar

1/4 cup melted butter

FOR FILLING:

1 3/4 pounds (28 oz) cream cheese

1 1/4 cups sugar

3/4 cup pumpkin purée

1/4 cup flour

1/4 teaspoon salt

1/4 teaspoon pumpkin pie spice

3/8 teaspoon ground ginger

Pinch ground nutmeg

3 eggs plus 1 egg yolk

1/4 cup heavy cream

Position rack in center of oven. Preheat oven to 350° F. Butter bottom and sides of a 10-inch springform pan.

In a medium bowl combine graham cracker crumbs and sugar; add melted butter and mix thoroughly. Press into prepared pan and set aside.

Combine cream cheese and sugar in mixing bowl. Using electric mixer set at medium speed, beat until smooth. Add pumpkin, flour, salt, and spices. Blend until well incorporated. Beat in eggs, egg yolk, and cream until thoroughly mixed. Pour batter into prepared springform pan.

Bake on center rack until firm around edges but center jiggles slightly when tapped, about 45 minutes. Cool on wire rack to room temperature, then remove pan sides and transfer cake to serving plate. Cover and refrigerate overnight before serving.

FRANGO® MINT CHOCOLATES

You need only pop a Frango® Mint Chocolate into your mouth to appreciate why people all over the world are passionately fond of this bite-sized chocolate morsel.

Created in the early 1900s by the Frederick Nelson Company, the confection was originally called a Franco. In 1929, Marshall Field's acquired Frederick Nelson and its popular candy. When General Franco and the Spanish Civil War hit the headlines in the 1930s, Field's changed the name from the Franco to the Frango®.

Field's candy kitchen, located in the famed downtown Chicago department store, produces more than 1.3 million pounds of Frango® chocolates each year. Over the years, the Frango® family has grown to include nine distinctive flavors. In addition, there are special holiday Frango®s at Christmas and Easter, to say nothing of Frango® mint pie, Frango® toppings for fruit and ice cream, and Frango® liqueurs.

Marshall Field's is a family institution. Memories of Christmas windows and of holiday trees in the elegant Walnut Room remain in the hearts of some Chicagoans all their lives. But the Frango® Mint Chocolate is more tangible than memory: It can and does go with its fans wherever they wander.

FRANGO® CHOCOLATE BROWNIES

MAKES 9 BROWNIES

❀

MOIST, FUDGY AND NUTTY, THESE SENSATIONAL BROWNIES WILL FILL YOUR KITCHEN WITH WONDERFUL AROMAS AS THEY BAKE.

1/2 cup (1 stick) unsalted butter, at room temperature

2 ounces unsweetened chocolate, finely chopped

2 large eggs, at room temperature

1 cup sugar

1 teaspoon vanilla extract

1/2 cup flour

1/8 teaspoon salt

1/2 cup coarsely chopped pecans

8 Frango® Mint Chocolates, chopped (about 1/2 cup)

Position rack in center of oven. Preheat to 350° F.

In heavy-bottomed medium saucepan over low heat, melt butter. Remove from heat, add chocolate, and stir until chocolate melts. Let mixture cool until tepid.

Place eggs in bowl. Using hand-held electric mixer set at medium speed, beat eggs until light and thickened, about 2 minutes. Beat in chocolate mixture and vanilla. Using rubber spatula, fold in flour and salt. Then fold in pecans and Frango®s. Spread batter evenly in buttered 8-inch square baking pan.

Bake on center oven rack until toothpick inserted halfway between center and edge of pan comes out with moist crumb, about 25 minutes. Do not overbake; brownies should be moist. Transfer brownies in pan to wire rack and cool completely.

Using sharp knife, cut brownies into 9 squares. Store in airtight container at room temperature up to 2 days.

STRAWBERRY SHORTCAKE

SERVES 6 TO 8

❋

THIS SHORTCAKE ALSO CAN BE MADE WITH BLUEBERRIES, BLACKBERRIES, WILD STRAWBERRIES, OR RASPBERRIES. OR FOR A QUICK DESSERT, USE LARGE SQUARES OF ANGEL FOOD CAKE OR SPONGE CAKE IN PLACE OF THE SHORTCAKES. ALTHOUGH MOST WOULD CONSIDER THIS TRADITIONAL MIDWESTERN DISH A DESSERT, TRY IT FOR AN IRRESISTIBLE BREAKFAST TREAT.

3 1/2 cups hulled, sliced strawberries

1/3 cup superfine sugar, divided

3 cups flour

4 teaspoons baking powder

1/2 teaspoon salt

1 teaspoon grated lemon zest

1/4 cup granulated sugar

2 tablespoons butter or margarine, at room temperature

1/2 cup vegetable shortening

1/2 cup half-and-half

1 egg

1 1/2 cups whipping cream, chilled

1 teaspoon vanilla extract

Place berries in bowl. Sprinkle half of the superfine sugar over top, cover, and refrigerate until needed.

Preheat oven to 425° F.

In a bowl combine flour, baking powder, salt, lemon zest, and granulated sugar. Using pastry blender or 2 knives, cut in butter and shortening until mixture is the consistency of fine crumbs. Add half-and-half and egg. Use pastry blender or electric mixer to mix.

On lightly floured work surface, roll out dough 1/2 inch thick. Using a floured biscuit cutter, cut out 3-inch rounds. You should have 6 to 8 rounds in all. Place rounds on non-stick baking sheet. Bake until golden brown, 13 to 15 minutes. Cool on wire rack.

While shortcakes are baking, pour cream into chilled bowl and beat to soft-peak stage.

While continuing to beat, sprinkle in vanilla and gradually add remaining superfine sugar, 2 tablespoons at a time. Incorporate until all sugar has been added and cream forms firm peaks.

   Split shortcakes horizontally and place on individual plates. Top the bottom half generously with whipped cream and berries and set top half at side. Serve immediately.

CHICAGO'S ELITE

The sumptuous dining of Chicago's elite in the late 1800s is typified by the dinner parties of Mrs. John Glessner of Prairie Avenue. The following passage from Mrs. Glessner's personal diary describes a dinner prepared at the Glessner home for the architect Mr. Richardson. A special thanks to the Chicago Architecture Foundation for permitting use of the excerpt!

We talked over the house and he then went with John to look over the lot. He was much pleased with that and said he would make us an ideal house. Mr. R. [Richardson] is the largest man I have ever seen.... [He was over six feet tall and weighed 370 pounds.] We invited him to dine here last evening—The time set was six o'clock—but they afterward postponed it to seven. We gave them [Mr. R. and Mr. and Mrs. Warder] a nice dinner. Asparagus, cream soup, Claret, Baked White Fish, New Orleans sauce, Cucumbers, Radishes, Spring Chicken, Peas, Gooseberry sauce, Pickles, Olives, Cheese, salad, Crackers, Almonds, Champagne, Strawberry Shortcake, Apricots, Cherries, Strawberries, Coffee. He enjoyed his dinner—and said ...the pie was the nicest thing he ever ate (the shortcake)....

CHAPTER 3

Prairie Appetizers

Light meals and party food made up of many small dishes go under different names in different cuisines. Tapas and hors d'oeuvres are just two examples. Now add to the list of party fare prairie appetizers, featuring classic ingredients of the prairie and other areas of the Midwest, combined in recipes for people who enjoy sampling an array of dishes. Put these recipes to work for you when assembling food for a crowd. Remember that some of them are flavorful enough to stand alone as a first course.

SMOKED TROUT CHEESECAKE WITH SWEET-AND-SOUR RED ONIONS

SERVES 10 TO 12

❋

MICHAEL HIGGINS, MANAGING CHEF OF MALDANER'S RESTAURANT IN SPRINGFIELD, ILLINOIS, BRINGS TOGETHER MANY LOCAL PRODUCTS IN HIS CREATIVE, UPSCALE STYLE. "FOOD IS MORE FUN TODAY, WITH MORE TASTES AND FLAVORS ON ONE PLATE. IT COMES TOGETHER LIKE GOOD MUSIC," SAYS CHEF HIGGINS. HERE IS ONE OF HIS CREATIONS. IT MAY BE SERVED AS AN APPETIZER, YET ITS PRESENTATION IS DRAMATIC ENOUGH TO BECOME THE CENTERPIECE FOR A BUFFET OF PÂTÉS, TERRINES, AND OTHER PARTY FOODS.

FOR CRUST:

1/2 cup roasted hazelnuts, skins removed, minced

6 tablespoons (3/4 stick) butter, at room temperature

FOR FILLING:

1 1/2 pounds (24 oz) cream cheese, cut into 1/2-inch cubes

6 eggs

2 cups sour cream

1/3 cup sifted flour

Grated zest of 1 lemon, 1/2 lime, and 1/2 orange

Juice of 1/2 lemon

1 1/2 cups flaked smoked trout or other smoked fish

1 cup minced green onions

1/4 teaspoon salt

1/2 teaspoon pepper

4 dashes Tabasco sauce

Preheat oven to 350° F.

To make crust, grease 10-inch springform pan. In bowl mix nuts with butter. Pat nut-butter mixture firmly and evenly onto bottom of prepared pan. Set aside.

To make filling, place cream cheese in large bowl and beat with electric mixer until soft and creamy. Blend in eggs, one at a time, beating after each addition until blended. Add sour cream, flour, lemon, lime and orange zest, and lemon juice; beat thoroughly. Stir in smoked trout, green onions, salt, pepper, and Tabasco. Pour cheese mixture into prepared pan.

FOR SWEET-AND-SOUR RED ONIONS:
1 cup each red wine vinegar and sugar
2 large red onions, sliced and separated into rings
2 tablespoons capers with brine

Bake 1 hour. Turn off heat and allow cheesecake to remain in oven for 1 hour longer. Cool to room temperature. Cover and chill overnight.

To make sweet-and-sour onions, mix vinegar and sugar in saucepan. Place over medium heat and simmer 5 minutes. Place onion and capers in bowl. Pour hot vinegar mixture over top and let stand at room temperature, stirring occasionally, 3 to 4 hours.

To serve, cut cheesecake into thin slices. Serve onions as a relish alongside.

ROLLMOPS

MAKES 12 ROLLMOPS

✲

ROLLMOPS MAKE A SUPERB APPETIZER OR BRUNCH DISH. THESE GERMAN SPECIALTIES ARE MADE OF PICKLED HERRING FILLETS ROLLED AROUND A DILL PICKLE AND ONION SLICES. THEY ARE NEARLY ALWAYS AVAILABLE IN GERMAN DELICATESSENS, THOSE DELIGHTFUL SHOPS THAT HAVE MADE SO MANY CONTRIBUTIONS TO THE WORLD OF CUISINE. PICTURE AN ARTISTICALLY DISPLAYED COUNTER OF COLD-SMOKED AND PICKLED FISH, SPICY SAUSAGES, WARM BREADS, AND CHEESES AND IMAGINE ALL THEIR AROMATIC CHARMS MINGLING. NOW YOU KNOW THE IRRESISTIBLE ATTRACTION OF A GERMAN DELI.

12 small fresh herring fillets, rinsed

2 cups cider vinegar

1 1/2 cups water

4 juniper berries

1/3 cup pickling spice

1/4 teaspoon pepper

2 bay leaves

1/4 cup German mustard

3 tablespoons drained capers

2 large onions, thinly sliced and separated into rings

3 large dill pickles, cut lengthwise into quarters

Place herring in a glass bowl and add water to cover. Refrigerate 24 hours, changing water twice. Drain herring; rinse under cold running water. Pat dry with paper towels. Feel with fingertips for any bones and remove.

In saucepan combine vinegar, water, juniper berries, pickling spice, pepper, and bay leaves. Bring to boil over medium heat. Reduce heat to low and simmer 4 minutes. Remove from heat and cool completely.

To assemble rollmops, lay fillets, skin sides down, on plate. Spread about 1 teaspoon of the mustard over each fillet. Sprinkle about 1/2 teaspoon of the capers on top, then scatter on a few onion rings. Roll up each herring fillet around a pickle slice and secure in place with toothpicks.

Layer rollmops in glass dish. Add additional onion rings and pour vinegar mixture over top. Cover with plastic wrap or aluminum foil and refrigerate at least 3 days before serving.

To serve, remove from dish with slotted spoon, set rollmops on plate, and sprinkle with remaining onion rings and capers.

SALMON CARPACCIO

SERVES 6

❋

MOST OFTEN MADE WITH THINLY SLICED, TENDER RAW BEEF, CARPACCIO ALSO CAN BE MADE WITH FILLET OF SALMON—ANOTHER HEARTLAND SPECIALTY. FOR THIS RECIPE IT'S IMPORTANT

TO TELL YOUR FISHMONGER THAT YOU NEED EXCEPTIONAL-LY FRESH FISH, SINCE IT IS TO BE EATEN RAW.

1/2-pound piece very fresh center-cut salmon
1/4 cup extra virgin olive oil
Freshly ground pepper
2 tablespoons capers with brine
6 tablespoons minced fresh parsley
6 tablespoons minced fresh cilantro
2 limes, thinly sliced
Toasted thin sourdough bread slices

Cut salmon into paper-thin slices; you should have 18 slices in all. Arrange 3 salmon slices on each chilled plate. Drizzle 2 teaspoons olive oil over salmon and sprinkle with pepper. Sprinkle 1 teaspoon capers with brine over salmon. On each plate arrange 1 tablespoon parsley on right side of salmon and 1 tablespoon cilantro on left side. Garnish with lime slices.

Serve chilled with toasted bread slices.

INDIVIDUAL PIZZAS

MAKES SIX 8-INCH PIZZAS

✻

INDIVIDUAL PIZZAS ARE CREATIVE APPETIZERS LIMITED ONLY BY ONE'S IMAGINATION. TWO SUGGESTED TOPPINGS FOLLOW. YOU CAN CREATE OTHERS BASED ON WHAT'S IN SEASON.

To make dough, in small bowl dissolve yeast and sugar in 1/4 cup of the warm water. Let stand until bubbly, 5 to 10 minutes.

Pour yeast mixture into large mixing bowl; stir in salt and oil. Mix in 1 cup of the flour, then stir in remaining warm water. Add remaining flour, 1 cup at a time, and continue to stir until dough is pliable.

FOR DOUGH:

1 package active dry yeast

1 1/2 teaspoons sugar

3/4 cup warm water (105° to 115° F)

1/2 teaspoon salt

2 tablespoons extra virgin olive oil

2 3/4 cups flour

6 ounces grated mozzarella cheese

Toppings (suggestions follow)

Turn dough out onto lightly floured surface and knead until smooth and elastic, about 8 minutes. Gather dough into ball. Place in oiled bowl and turn to oil top. Cover bowl loosely with aluminum foil and let rise in warm, draft-free area until doubled in volume, about 1 hour.

Meanwhile, preheat oven to 475° F. Lightly brush 2 or 3 baking sheets with oil.

Punch down dough and divide into 8 equal pieces.

On lightly floured board pat each piece of dough into rounds 8 inches in diameter. Arrange 3 or 4 dough rounds on each baking sheet.

Sprinkle each dough round with an equal amount of the mozzarella cheese. Decorate each pizza with one of the following toppings or one of your own design.

Bake until cheese melts and crust edges are golden brown, 10 to 12 minutes.

For Goat Cheese and Sun-Dried Tomato Topping: For 1 pizza, thinly slice 1 1/2 ounces goat cheese and arrange atop mozzarella layer. Sprinkle with 2 sun-dried tomatoes packed in olive oil (do not drain), chopped, and 1/4 teaspoon fennel seed. Top with 2 tablespoons pine nuts, lightly toasted. Bake as directed.

For Eggplant and Mushroom Topping: For 1 pizza, in skillet over medium heat, melt 1 tablespoon butter with 1 tablespoon extra virgin olive oil. Add 3 eggplant slices (each 1/4 inch thick by 3 inches in diameter) and sauté, turning once, 2 minutes on each side. Sprinkle with 1/2 teaspoon dried oregano. Arrange eggplant slices atop mozzarella layer. Top with 1 large fresh white mushroom, thinly sliced. Sprinkle with 1 tablespoon grated Asiago cheese. Bake as directed.

CHEESE COUNTRY, U.S.A.

Although the fields and farms of Wisconsin produce an abundance of meats, vegetables, and fruits, cheese still reigns supreme. The old cliche, "Just say cheese," applies to more than two hundred Wisconsin cheese varieties, the result of a 150-year tradition of cheese making that reflects the state's rich ethnic background.

Swiss, Dutch, German, Scandinavian, French, and Italian immigrants to the state reproduced the classic cheeses of their homelands. This diversity produced Swiss, provolone, Roquefort, Brie, Edam, Gouda, Cheddar and Muenster, along with such Wisconsin originals as Colby and brick. The state now supplies 50 percent of the nation's cheese, 20 percent of its milk, and 25 percent of its butter. No wonder Wisconsin license plates boast the slogan *America's Dairyland*.

The state's cheese empire began as a cottage industry in the mid-1800s. It was in 1864, when Chester Hazen built his cheese factory in Loadoga, that Wisconsin cheese production truly began to grow. At that time, most people felt that cheese couldn't be made on a large scale and that old Chester was doomed to fail. They called his factory Hazen's Folly. But thanks to aggressive ideas and production methods, Chester's operation grew and by the end of the first year he was using milk from three hundred cows. So-called Hazen's Folly helped place Wisconsin on the road to becoming the nation's leading cheese producer. Today, the labels *Wisconsin Grade A* and *Wisconsin State Brand* guarantee some of the country's finest cheese.

HICKORY-SMOKED SWISS CHEESE

MAKES 1/2 POUND

✳

PURE MIDWESTERN GOLD—CHEESE—IS KING IN WISCONSIN, THE LEADER OF THE NATION'S DAIRY INDUSTRIES. THE CHEESE ABSORBS THE SMOKE FLAVOR QUICKLY, PRODUCING A DELICIOUS FARE FOR PARTIES OR SNACKS. BE SURE THAT THE HEAT IS LOW ENOUGH SO THAT THE CHEESE DOES NOT MELT DURING THE SMOKING PROCESS.

1/2 pound Wisconsin Swiss cheese
2 cups hickory or applewood chips soaked 30 minutes in water to cover and drained

Prepare smoker, following manufacturer's instructions. Fill coal pan two-thirds full with charcoal and heat coals until hot and ashen. Sprinkle coals with hickory chips. Have water pan ready with hot water. Using pot holders, set pan on rack.

Place unwrapped cheese on sheet of aluminum foil large enough to encase. Place cheese on top rack of smoker. Bring sides of foil up slightly, but leave cheese exposed to smoke. Cover smoker and smoke cheese for 20 minutes.

Remove cover and immediately refrigerate cheese for 30 minutes.

Serve at room temperature.

WILD MUSHROOM STRUDEL

SERVES 6

✳

CHEF MILOS CIHELKA OF THE GOLDEN MUSHROOM RESTAURANT IN SOUTHFIELD, MICHIGAN, IS THE RECIPIENT OF MANY PRESTIGIOUS CULINARY AWARDS. HE WAS MANAGER OF THE 1988 MICHIGAN CULINARY TEAM, WHICH WON NUMEROUS NATIONAL AND INTERNATIONAL COMPETITIONS. THIS RECIPE EXEMPLIFIES CIHELKA'S WORLD-CLASS CULINARY STATURE.

1/4 cup (1/2 stick) butter

3 tablespoons shallots, chopped

2 1/2 quarts fresh wild mushrooms, sliced

3 tablespoons flour

1/3 cup dry sherry

1/3 cup whipping cream

Salt and pepper, to taste

1/4 cup chopped fresh parsley

4 sheets phyllo dough

1/3 cup clarified butter, melted and cooled

In saucepan over medium heat, melt butter. Add shallots and sauté but do not allow to brown. Add mushrooms and sauté until all juices evaporate.

Dust shallots and mushrooms with flour, and stir to prevent lumping. Add sherry, cream, salt and pepper, and cook a little longer until mixture thickens. Remove from heat; spread on pan to cool and add parsley.

Preheat oven to 400° F.

Place 1 phyllo sheet on clean towel or napkin (keep remaining sheets of phyllo covered so they do not dry out). Brush with some of the melted clarified butter. Place another sheet on top and brush again. Repeat until all sheets are stacked. Facing long side of phyllo stack, place cooled mushroom mixture along edge of stack nearest you. Grasp towel and lift up edge of phyllo stack so it covers filling. Now roll up phyllo away from you, encasing the filling snugly in the phyllo as you go. Using towel, lift roll and place seam down on parchment-lined baking sheet. Brush with melted butter. Bake until browned and crispy, 25 to 30 minutes. Slice into serving pieces and serve warm.

WILD MUSHROOMS

Starting in late April and early May, mushroom foragers flock to the Midwest countryside. Because the weather is still cold and damp, mushroom hunting often means scrambling through leaves and twigs left wet by spring showers. Of course, outdoor markets, specialty food shops, and some super-markets also are sources for a number of varieties of fresh wild mushrooms, including chanterelles, morels, oyster, and porcini (cèpes). But fresh wild mushrooms are worth the effort.

Wisconsin, Michigan, Illinois, Indiana, and Iowa all have quiet woods where one can hunt the wild mushroom. The selection varies according to soil and forest conditions.

Caution: **Some varieties of mushrooms are toxic, capable of produc-ing gastric distress and other symptoms and, in some cases, even death. Never eat or even taste a wild mushroom that you cannot posi-tively identify as edible or that has not been so identified by an experi-enced collector.**

When cooking fresh wild mushrooms, be sure to inspect and clean them thoroughly. Check for grit and bugs, which often hide in the crevices and flanges of the caps. Wild mushrooms have a flavor both delicate and intense, a far cry from that of cultivated varieties.

BITE-SIZED PORK PASTIES

MAKES 18 PASTIES

❋

CORNISH MINERS, IMMIGRANTS TO THE UPPER PENINSULA OF MICHIGAN DURING THE 1870S, ARE CREDITED WITH INTRODUCING THE DELICIOUS LITTLE VEGETABLE-AND-MEAT PACKAGES CALLED PASTIES (RHYMES WITH NASTIES). FRESH FROM THE OVEN AND CARRIED IN A SHIRT POCKET, PASTIES KEPT THE MEN WARM ON THEIR WAY TO WORK IN THE MORNING. AT NOON, THE SAVORY PASTRIES WERE EASILY REHEATED ON A SHOVEL HELD OVER A MINER'S LAMP.

TODAY, THESE HEARTY, NOURISHING PIES CAN BE MADE AHEAD OF TIME IN BATCHES, STORED IN THE FREEZER, AND REHEATED IN THE MICROWAVE IN MINUTES. WHETHER AS A FAMILY MEAL, A HEARTY APPETIZER, A CHILD'S LUNCH, OR A QUICK SATISFYING SNACK, PASTIES—LARGE OR BITE-SIZED—ARE EASY TO MAKE AND FUN TO EAT.

SIZE YOUR PASTIES ACCORDING TO HOW YOU PLAN TO SERVE THEM. HALF-MOON PASTIES CAN BE MADE INTO TINY TWO-BITE MORSELS OR CAN BE PREPARED THE SIZE OF A SANDWICH. TRADITIONALLY SERVED PIPING HOT WITH WISCONSIN BEER.

FOR PASTRY:

4 cups flour

1/2 teaspoon salt

1/2 teaspoon baking powder

1 cup (8 oz) vegetable shortening, at room temperature, cut into 1/2-inch pieces

1/2 to 3/4 cup water, ice cold

FOR FILLING:

1 cup coarsely chopped onion

2 1/2 cups peeled, diced potato

1 cup grated carrot

1 1/2 pounds pork loin, finely diced

3/4 teaspoon salt

1/4 teaspoon pepper

1 egg, lightly beaten

In a food processor fitted with steel blade, combine flour, salt, baking powder, and shortening. Using on-off pulses, process until ingredients are mixed and mixture is grainlike in appearance. With machine running, add ice water through tube, 1/4 cup at a time, until dough ball forms.

Alternatively, in deep bowl, combine flour, salt, baking powder, and shortening. Using pastry blender or 2 knives, cut in shortening until mixture is grainlike in appearance. Add ice water, 1/4 cup at a time, working it in with pastry blender or 2 knives.

Gather dough into ball, cover with aluminum foil and refrigerate 45 minutes.

Meanwhile, preheat oven to 400° F.

To make filling, in bowl toss together onion, potato, carrot, pork, salt, and pepper.

Remove dough from refrigerator and divide into 18 equal pieces. On lightly floured work surface, roll out each dough piece into 6-inch round. (Each will be a little more than 1/8 inch thick.) Mound a heaping 1/3 cup filling on half of dough round. Moisten edges of round with water, fold in half to enclose filling and crimp edges together. Pasties will look like semicircles.

Arrange pasties on 2 ungreased baking sheets. Cut 2 slits each about 1 inch long in top of each pastie. Brush lightly with beaten egg. Bake until golden brown, about 30 minutes.

Serve hot.

GAME SAUSAGE WITH SMOKED APPLES, GRILLED ONIONS, AND MAPLE CREAM SAUCE

SERVES 6 TO 8

❋

PETER GEORGE OF PETER'S RESTAURANT IN INDIANAPOLIS, INDIANA, HAS GRACIOUSLY CONTRIBUTED THIS CREATIVE AND DELICIOUS RECIPE.

6 Winesap apples

FOR GAME SAUSAGE:

Juice and zest of 1 orange

2 fresh sage sprigs

2 fresh thyme sprigs

15 juniper berries

20 peppercorns

1/4 cup brandy

3 tablespoons salt

1 pound venison, cut into 1-inch cubes

1 1/2 pounds lean pork, cut into 1-inch cubes

1/2 pound fat back, cut into 1-inch cubes

2 smoked apples, chopped

To make smoked apples, prepare smoker according to manufacturer's directions. Cut apples in half. Place flesh side down on smoker rack. Cover smoker and smoke 15 to 20 minutes. Remove apples and cool. Seed, peel, and thinly slice. Set aside.

To make sausage, in large bowl place orange juice and zest, herb sprigs, juniper berries, peppercorns, brandy, salt, meats, and chopped apples. Toss well and let stand 45 minutes.

Pass sausage mixture through sausage grinder fitted with large grinding plate.

Remove plate and blade and fit sausage grinder with funnel for stuffing sausage casings. Stuff casings and tie off to form sausages.

Bring large saucepan three- fourths full of water to boil. Add sausage, reduce heat to low, and poach sausages 20 minutes. Drain well and let cool completely.

To make sauce, in saucepan combine maple syrup, sugar, stock, and apple juice. Place over high heat and bring to boil, stirring to dissolve sugar. Cook over medium-high heat until reduced by one fourth. Add cream and again cook over medium-high

FOR MAPLE CREAM SAUCE:

1/2 cup maple syrup

1/4 cup firmly packed brown sugar

1 cup stock

3/4 cup apple juice

4 cups whipping cream

2 red onions, sliced

Salt and pepper to taste

heat until reduced by one fourth. Season to taste. (Sauce may be made in advance and set aside during preparation of sausages.)

Grill sausage and onions until browned. Garnish with remaining smoked apples. Serve immediately with sauce (reheated if necessary).

THE NAUVOO CHEESE COMPANY

Nestled on the banks of the Mississippi lies Nauvoo, Illinois, known both as the launching site of the Mormon Trek in 1846 and as the home of one of the Heartland's myriad of food industries, the Nauvoo Cheese Company.

Nauvoo blue cheese, which has gained national acclaim, had its origin in the 1920s when Prohibition resulted in the conversion of the sixty to seventy wine cellars that had been used for wine production to aging of Roquefort-style cheese. The substitution of cow's milk for sheep's milk created Nauvoo blue. Thus, the rich mine of wine cellars found a new use, and several generations of cheese lovers have reaped the benefits ever since.

Both the citizens of Nauvoo and the forty-seven employees of the Nauvoo Cheese Company are extremely proud of their products. That pride was further justified when in 1991 Nauvoo blue and Nauvoo Gorgonzola became the first blue-veined cheeses to merit the prestigious Gold Medal Award from the Chefs of America Awards Foundation, an organization dedicated to identifying and certifying North America's finest food and beverage products.

Nauvoo blue cheese possesses an incredibly clean, fresh taste, and its creamy texture makes it perfect for spreading or blending. It is also wonderful crumbled into salads, sauces, and other dishes for which both Roqueforts and blue cheeses are famous. If you are passing through Nauvoo, be certain to pay a visit to the Nauvoo Cheese Company. Elsewhere, look for Nauvoo blue and Nauvoo Gorgonzola for an insurmountable taste sensation.

SHERRY-BLUE CHEESE CROCK

SERVES 6

❋

SERVE THIS FLAVORFUL CHEESE SPREAD WITH PICKLED SQUASH AND PUMPKIN (SEE PAGE 54). SPREAD THE CHEESE ON CRUDITÉS SUCH AS GREEN ONIONS AND PEPPER AND CARROT STRIPS, AS WELL AS CRACKERS OR THIN SLICES OF WHOLE-GRAIN BREAD.

1 pound blue cheese, preferably Nauvoo blue, at room temperature

1/2 pound cream cheese, at room temperature, cut into 1/2-inch pieces

1 small onion, minced

3 tablespoons dry sherry

Pickled Squash and Pumpkin (recipe follows)

Crumble blue cheese into mixing bowl. Add cream cheese, onion, and sherry. Using the back of a wooden spoon, blend ingredients together until smooth. Alternatively, use food processor fitted with a steel blade to mix ingredients together.

Mound blue cheese into 2 1/2- to 3-cup crock. Cover and refrigerate 30 minutes before serving.

PICKLED SQUASH AND PUMPKIN

MAKES ABOUT 6 CUPS

✺

ALTHOUGH THIS VEGETABLE DISH IS A TRADITIONAL ACCOMPANIMENT TO SHERRY-BLUE CHEESE CROCK (SEE PAGE 53) AND OTHER SAVORIES ON MIDWEST HORS D'OEUVRE TRAYS, IT ALSO GOES WELL WITH POULTRY AND MEAT.

HERE'S A HINT FOR ACCURATE MEASUREMENT OF THE CUT SQUASH AND PUMPKIN: FILL A 4-CUP MEASURE WITH 2 1/2 CUPS WATER. ADD SQUASH OR PUMPKIN, PEELED AND CUT INTO PIECES. WHEN WATER REACHES THE 4-CUP MARK, YOU WILL HAVE 1 1/2 CUPS OF THE VEGETABLES. DRAIN BEFORE USING.

1 1/2 cups cubed, peeled pumpkin (3/4-inch cubes)

1 1/2 cups sliced, peeled yellow (butternut) squash (1/2-inch thick slices)

2 cups distilled white vinegar

2 cups sugar

1 onion, thinly sliced

1 teaspoon ground cinnamon or 8 cinnamon sticks

1/2 teaspoon each ground cloves, celery seed, and salt

In saucepan combine pumpkin and yellow squash. Add water to cover and bring to boil over medium heat. Reduce heat to low and simmer 15 minutes. Drain well and place in heatproof bowl.

In saucepan combine vinegar, sugar, onion, cinnamon, cloves, celery seed, and salt. Bring mixture to boil over medium heat. Reduce to low and simmer 3 minutes. Pour hot vinegar mixture over squash and pumpkin. Cool, cover, and refrigerate overnight. Serve, using slotted spoon.

CHAPTER 4

The Stockpot

What keeps many people from making soup at home is time. With a little foresight, however, soups can become a staple of your weekly meal plans.

For instance, you can start soup the night before you serve it. Not only is this approach more convenient, but it also allows the flavors to meld. Leftover soup can be stored in the refrigerator or freezer and served later as a hearty lunch. Soups are an integral part of Heartland cuisine.

CHERRY CAPITAL OF THE WORLD

Michigan's fruit belt, which stretches across the northern Lower Peninsula, is home to scores of orchards that supply the cooks of Michigan and the nation with apples, cherries, peaches, plums, grapes, and pears. Paula Red apples and Red Haven peaches fill pie shells, salad bowls, and jelly jars. Raspberries, blackberries, and blueberries abound; blueberries and cherries are shipped dried all over the country. Wild thimbleberries, Concord grapes, and Italian purple plums also contribute to the jelly and jam market.

But the real glory of Michigan fruits is the tart red cherry. The state provides 75 percent of the nation's sour pie cherries. Traverse City, Michigan, the Cherry Capital of the World, hosts the National Cherry Festival in July. One of the highlights of the celebrations is a cherry smorgasbord luncheon, replete with soups (see page 57), entrées, salads, cakes, ice cream, cookies, and, of course, pies.

COLD CHERRY SOUP

SERVES 6

✻

SCANDINAVIAN IMMIGRANTS BROUGHT THE CONCEPT OF FRUIT SOUPS WITH THEM TO THE HEARTLAND. THEY USED EITHER FRESH OR DRIED CHERRIES FOR THIS SOUP, BUT YOU CAN USE FRESH, DRIED, OR CANNED. TRADITIONALLY, THE SOUP WAS SERVED COLD AS A DESSERT COURSE, BUT IT IS EQUALLY DELICIOUS HOT. AND IN THE SUMMER WHEN FRESH CHERRIES ARE PLENTIFUL, IT MAKES A PARTICULARLY REFRESHING COLD SOUP COURSE. WHETHER SERVED HOT OR CHILLED, AS A SOUP COURSE OR AS DESSERT, THIS SOUP ADDS ZEST AND COLOR TO A MEAL. IT CAN BE PREPARED UP TO TWO DAYS IN ADVANCE AND REFRIGERATED UNTIL SERVING.

1 1/2 pounds tart cherries, pitted and puréed

2 1/2 cups water

1 1/2 cups dry red wine

3 tablespoons sugar, or to taste

1/2 teaspoon ground cinnamon

1/4 teaspoon ground nutmeg

2 tablespoons cornstarch

1 cup whipping cream, whipped

In saucepan, stir together cherry purée, water, wine, sugar, cinnamon, and nutmeg. Bring soup to boil over medium heat. Cover, reduce heat to low, and simmer 8 to 10 minutes.

Remove about 1/2 cup soup to small bowl and whisk in cornstarch. Return mixture to soup and cook over medium heat, stirring often, 3 minutes. The soup will thicken slightly.

Taste soup and adjust seasonings. Cool. Place soup in a glass bowl, cover, and refrigerate until ready to serve.

At serving time, ladle soup into individual bowls and garnish with dollops of whipped cream.

CORN CHOWDER WITH CORN ON THE COB

SERVES 6

❋

QUICK TO FIX AND HEARTY ENOUGH FOR A MAIN DISH, THIS HEARTY CORN CHOWDER WILL BECOME A STANDBY. SERVE ALL YEAR ROUND, USING FRESHLY PICKED CORN IN SUMMERTIME OR FROZEN CORN FOR A WARM, SATISFYING SOUP TO WARD OFF WINTER'S CHILL.

3 slices bacon, cut into 1-inch pieces

1 large onion, minced

2 cups corn kernels, fresh or frozen, thawed

1 can (15 oz) creamed corn

2 large potatoes, peeled, boiled until tender, and cut into 1/2-inch cubes

2 cups chicken stock

3 large ears corn, shucked and cut in half

2 cups milk or half-and-half

1/2 teaspoon salt

1/2 teaspoon white pepper

In large saucepan over medium heat, fry together bacon and onion stirring often, about 5 minutes. Add corn kernels, creamed corn, potatoes, stock, and corn pieces. Reduce heat to low and simmer until corn pieces are cooked, about 10 minutes. Stir in milk and heat through. Add salt and pepper to taste.

To serve, place 1 piece of corn in each soup bowl. Ladle hot soup into bowls. Serve piping hot.

SEVEN GREENS SOUP

SERVES 8

✹

IN 1929, MR. AND MRS. JOHN BODER OPENED BODER'S-ON-THE-RIVER IN MEQUON, WISCONSIN. SIXTY-THREE YEARS AND FOUR GENERATIONS OF BODER FAMILY LATER, THIS COUNTRY RESTAU-RANT HAS BECOME A DINING TRADITION NOTED FOR DISHES OF ELEGANT SIMPLICITY, IN-CLUDING THIS SOUP.

4 cups chicken stock

7 tablespoons (7/8 stick) butter

1/4 cup finely chopped cabbage

1/4 cup finely chopped red leaf lettuce

1/4 cup finely chopped romaine or iceberg lettuce

1/4 cup finely chopped spinach

1/4 cup chopped fresh parsley

1/4 cup alfalfa sprouts

1 small garlic clove, crushed

6 tablespoons flour

1 cup half-and-half

Salt and pepper, to taste

Chives, for garnish

Pour stock into large saucepan over medium heat and bring to simmer. Meanwhile, in large skillet over medium heat, melt 4 tablespoons of the butter. Add cabbage, lettuces, spinach, parsley, alfalfa sprouts, and garlic and sauté until wilted. Add sautéed veg-etables to simmering stock and continue to cook gently.

While vegetables are simmering, melt remaining 3 tablespoons butter in saucepan. Stir in 3 tablespoons flour and cook, stirring occasionally, until mixture does not stick to sides of pan, 3 to 5 minutes. Stir flour mixture into stock. Simmer, stirring, until soup thickens.

Stir in half-and-half and season with salt and pepper. Serve hot, garnished with finely chopped chives.

THE MORTON, ILLINOIS, PUMPKIN FESTIVAL

Morton, Illinois, is the Pumpkin Capital of the World and home to the annual Morton Pumpkin Festival, which has been celebrated since 1966. In Morton the festivities associated with pumpkin worship are as respectably and sincerely appreciated as those of any Super Bowl.

Each fall for approximately ten weeks, truckload after truckload—up to seventy-five daily—roll into Morton. Over four thousand acres of pumpkin-laden fields lie within a 50-mile radius of the town. Pumpkins are processed at the Nestle-Carnation Libby plant into millions of cases of canned pumpkin. If you purchase canned pumpkin in the United States, it likely was canned in Morton, Illinois.

The Pumpkin Festival is a four-day event that involves a tremendous variety of activities and a particularly wonderful array of foods, from Heartland pork chop sandwiches to great pumpkin cookies and even pumpkin pancakes. There are ingenious pumpkin-decorating entries and kids of all ages join in a search for the Great Pumpkin.

PUMPKIN SOUP

SERVES 6 TO 8

✻

THE PUMPKIN HAS A LONG HISTORY IN THE UNITED STATES. NATIVE AMERICANS AND GENERA-TIONS OF SETTLERS DEPENDED ON ITS NUTRITIONAL VALUE AND VERSATILITY IN THEIR DAILY LIVES. LOW IN CALORIES (1/2 CUP IS A MERE 24 CALORIES) AND RICH IN VITAMIN A, PUMPKIN IS MUCH MORE THAN JUST A PRETTY FACE.

THIS SOUP IS PARTICULARLY ATTRACTIVE WHEN SERVED IN A HOLLOWED-OUT PUMPKIN. TO USE A PUMPKIN AS A TUREEN, SELECT A MEDIUM-SIZED PUMPKIN. CUT OFF 2 INCHES FROM THE TOP. THEN CUT A SLICE 1/4 INCH THICK OFF THE BOTTOM TO HELP BALANCE THE SQUASH. SCOOP OUT AND DISCARD SOFT MEMBRANES, STRINGS, AND SEEDS. WHEN READY TO SERVE, POUR SOUP INTO PUMPKIN AND BRING TO THE TABLE.

1/4 cup (1/2 stick) butter or margarine

1 onion, minced

1 can (29 oz) pumpkin purée

3 cups chicken stock

1/2 teaspoon salt

1/2 teaspoon ground cinnamon

1/4 teaspoon each ground mace, ground allspice, and ground ginger

2 cups buttermilk

1/4 teaspoon freshly grated nutmeg

In large heavy saucepan over medium heat, melt butter. Add onion and sauté, stirring often, until translucent, about 5 minutes. Stir in pumpkin purée, stock, salt, cinnamon, mace, allspice, and ginger. Simmer uncovered 10 minutes.

Stir in buttermilk and continue cooking until heated through. Sprinkle nutmeg over top and serve piping hot.

TOMATO SOUP WITH FLOATING POPCORN

SERVES 6

❋

THIS UPDATED VERSION OF AN ALL-TIME FAVORITE SOUP FEATURES A SURPRISE TOPPING STRAIGHT FROM THE FARMLANDS OF THE GREAT PLAINS: POPCORN! HAVE A BOWL OF POPCORN ON THE TABLE FOR EXTRA HELPINGS.

3 tablespoons butter or margarine

1 tablespoon extra virgin olive oil

1 onion, minced

1/2 cup chopped celery

8 large tomatoes, peeled and chopped

3 cups chicken stock

1 can (16 oz) stewed tomatoes, including juice

1 tablespoon cider vinegar

1/2 teaspoon each salt, celery salt, dried basil, and dried thyme

1/4 teaspoon pepper

1 teaspoon honey

3 cups popped popcorn, plus extra for serving

In stockpot or large saucepan over medium heat, melt butter with oil. Add onion and celery and sauté until tender, about 5 minutes. Mix in chopped tomatoes, stock, stewed tomatoes, vinegar, salt, celery salt, basil, thyme, pepper, and honey. Bring to a boil, reduce heat to low, cover partially, and simmer 20 minutes. Remove from heat and cool slightly.

Working in 2 or 3 batches, in blender or food processor fitted with steel blade, purée soup. Return to clean pot and reheat to serving temperature.

Ladle soup into deep soup bowls. Float popcorn on top. Bring to table hot. Offer extra popcorn on the side.

OXTAIL SOUP

SERVES 8

✳

ORIGINALLY, OXTAILS WERE TRULY "FROM THE OX" AND WERE AVAILABLE IN BUTCHER SHOPS THROUGHOUT THE HEARTLAND STATES. TODAY, THE TERM GENERALLY REFERS TO BEEF OR VEAL TAIL. WHILE QUITE BONY AND SOMETIMES TOUGH, OXTAILS MAKE A BASE FOR AN EXTREMELY FLAVORFUL SOUP ONCE THEY HAVE BEEN LONG-COOKED WITH VEGETABLES, HERBS, AND SPICES. THIS SOUP, POPULARIZED IN THE MIDWEST BY EARLY ENGLISH SETTLERS, IS EVEN BETTER SERVED THE SECOND DAY AFTER YOU MAKE IT.

1/4 cup (1/2 stick) butter or margarine

2 tablespoons canola oil

3 cloves garlic, minced

2 leeks, white part only, sliced

2 1/2 pounds oxtails, rinsed and patted dry

2 tablespoons flour

1 can (16 oz) tomatoes, including juice, or 5 tomatoes, peeled and chopped

4 celery stalks, sliced

4 cups beef stock

1/2 teaspoon each salt, dried thyme, and dried basil

3 large bay leaves

1/4 teaspoon ground cloves

2 cups water

In large heavy pot over medium heat, melt butter with oil. Add garlic, leeks, and oxtails. Sprinkle with flour and cook, stirring often, until flour is absorbed, about 5 minutes.

Stir in tomatoes, celery, stock, salt, thyme, basil, bay leaves, and cloves. Simmer uncovered until meat is fork tender, about 1 hour. Add the water if soup is too thick.

Remove and discard bay leaves. Skim off any fat on surface. Divide oxtails equally among deep soup bowls. Ladle hot soup into bowls and serve immediately.

SPINACH AND CAULIFLOWER SOUP

SERVES 6

❋

DURING WINTER WHEN OTHER FRESH VEGETABLES ARE SCARCE, SPINACH AND CAULIFLOWER ARE AT THEIR PEAK IN MOST MARKETS. THEY JOIN FORCES HERE FOR AN UNLIKELY YET INTRIGUING COMBINATION OF TEXTURES AND FLAVORS. THE SWIRLING DESIGN OF THE FINISHED SOUP IS A VISUAL DELIGHT.

FOR CAULIFLOWER SOUP:

2 cups chopped, cooked cauliflower

1/2 teaspoon each salt and ground ginger

1/4 teaspoon each white pepper and ground nutmeg

1 cup half-and-half

3 tablespoons butter or margarine

1 1/2 tablespoons cornstarch

1 1/2 cups chicken stock

6 fresh cilantro or parsley sprigs

FOR SPINACH SOUP:

3 tablespoons butter

1 large onion, minced

4 cups spinach leaves

2 cups chicken stock

1/2 teaspoon each salt and dried dill weed

1/4 teaspoon pepper

1 cup half-and-half

To make cauliflower soup, in food processor fitted with steel blade, combine cauliflower, salt, ginger, pepper, nutmeg, and 1/4 cup of the half-and-half. Purée until smooth. Set aside.

In large saucepan over medium heat, melt butter. Whisk in cornstarch and continue whisking until it is absorbed. Slowly whisk in chicken stock and simmer 5 minutes. Stir in puréed cauliflower and heat 3 minutes. Add remaining half-and-half and simmer about 3 minutes until slightly thickened and smooth.

To make spinach soup, in large heavy saucepan over medium heat, melt butter. Add onion and sauté, stirring occasionally, until tender, about 5 minutes. Add spinach, mix well, and sauté 2 minutes. Stir in chicken stock and simmer 5 minutes. Remove from heat.

Transfer spinach mixture to food processor fitted with steel blade and purée until smooth. Place purée in clean saucepan and reheat. Simmer over low heat 5 minutes. Stir in half-and-half and heat to serving temperature.

To serve, ladle hot spinach soup into soup bowl. Ladle hot cauliflower soup into center of spinach soup. With knife, swirl cauliflower soup decoratively into spinach soup. Bring to table hot.

SALMON CHOWDER

SERVES 6

❋

GENEROUS CHUNKS OF SALMON AND VEGETABLES IN A LUSCIOUS BROTH TO SATISFY THE SOUL, AS WELL AS THE APPETITE, MAKE THIS CHOWDER SPECIAL.

FOR THE BEST FISH STOCK, USE FISH SCRAPS—HEADS AND TRIMMINGS—WHICH MOST FISH-MONGERS WILL SELL FOR LITTLE OR NOTHING. AVOID FAT-RICH OR OILY FISH WHEN MAKING THIS BROTH.

To make fish stock, place fish bones in large heavy pot or stockpot in water. Add onion, celery, wine, pepper-corns, parsley, and bay leaf. Add water to barely cover.

Bring to simmer over medium heat, cover partially, and simmer 45 minutes.

Skim any scum from stock and strain through a double layer of cheesecloth. You should have 2 to 2 1/2 cups. If you are not using stock immediately, pour into con-

FOR FISH STOCK:

1 1/2 pounds white fish bones

1 large onion, chopped

2 celery stalks, sliced

1 cup dry white wine, preferably a Heartland wine

6 peppercorns

3 fresh parsley sprigs

1 large bay leaf

FOR CHOWDER:

1/4 cup (1/2 stick) butter or margarine

1 onion, minced

2 celery stalks, sliced

1 carrot, peeled and sliced

1 1/2 pounds salmon fillet, cut into 1-inch pieces

1 cup fresh or frozen, thawed corn kernels

1 can (8 oz) chopped tomatoes, with their liquid

1/2 teaspoon salt

1/4 teaspoon each ground ginger and white pepper

1/2 cup chopped fresh chives or wild onions

tainer, cover, and refrigerate up to 2 days or freeze up to 1 month.

To make chowder, in large heavy saucepan over medium heat, melt butter. Add onion, celery, and carrot and sauté, stirring often, about 5 minutes. Add salmon, corn, tomatoes, salt, ginger, pepper, and 2 cups stock. Cover partially and simmer 20 minutes.

Ladle chowder into deep bowls. Sprinkle with chives and serve immediately.

SPLIT PEA SOUP WITH HAM

SERVES 8

✳

SMALL ROUND PEAS GROWN ESPECIALLY FOR DRYING ARE KNOWN AS FIELD PEAS. THEY ARE USUALLY SPLIT ALONG A NATURAL SEAM, HENCE THE NAME SPLIT PEAS. SPLIT PEA SOUP IS TRADITIONALLY ASSOCIATED WITH DUTCH CUISINE AND IS A POPULAR DISH ON WINTER EVENINGS IN MANY MIDWESTERN DUTCH, SCANDINAVIAN, AND GERMAN COMMUNITIES.

THE TASTE OF THIS SOUP ACTUALLY IMPROVES IF IT SITS OVERNIGHT IN A COVERED BOWL IN THE REFRIGERATOR.

10 cups (2 1/2 quarts) water
2 cups dried yellow or green split peas, rinsed
3/4 pound smoked ham, cubed, or 1 meaty cooked ham bone
2 onions, minced
2 large carrots, sliced
2 large bay leaves
1/2 teaspoon dried thyme
1/2 teaspoon dried marjoram
Salt and white pepper, to taste

In soup pot or other large pot, stir together the water and peas. Add ham pieces or bone, onions, carrots, thyme, marjoram, bay leaves, salt, and pepper. Bring to boil. Reduce heat to low, cover, and simmer 2 to 2 1/2 hours. The split peas should be quite soft.

Taste and adjust seasonings. If using ham bone, remove it and cut away meat. Discard bone, cut meat into chunks, and return to soup. Remove and discard bay leaves.

If you want a creamy soup, divide into 3 batches and purée, one batch at a time, in blender or food processor fitted with steel blade. Return purée to clean pot and reheat to serving temperature. Serve hot.

CHAPTER 5

The
Breadbasket

The Midwest table almost always includes at least one serving of carbohydrate-rich grain in the form of breads and other baked goods. The fertile soil of the Great Plains yields huge crops of wheat, rye, corn, oats, and such exotic near-grains as wild rice. Many of these harvests go into making the breads that grace meals in the Heartland and all over the country.

All the cereal grains have a long history in the region. The first settlers stirred cracked corn into stews and made thick morning porridges from whole oats. As farms were established, wheat and wheat flour predominated in the kitchen. And today, farmers in Iowa grow most of the nation's oats. Chippewa and Menominee Indians in northern Wisconsin harvested wild rice from their canoes and lived off it during the bitter winters.

It is no wonder the Heartland's nickname is The Nation's Breadbasket. Whether baked with yeast, salt, and water into a crusty, hearty loaf, or with butter, eggs, and sugar into a sweet cake, just-ground flour has a marvelous taste. Throughout the Midwest, small family-run mills and bakeries produce baked goods with a distinctive taste that comes from truly fresh flour grown on some of the richest soils in the world.

Baked goods from the Midwest and their unique use of locally grown grains and other ingredients—fruits, nuts, cheese, vegetable—contribute to the flavor profile of the Heartland breadbasket.

LIMPA BREAD

MAKES 1 LOAF

✳

INTRODUCED INTO HEARTLAND CUISINE BY SCANDINAVIAN IMMIGRANTS, THIS FRAGRANT
BREAD HIGHLIGHTS TWO FAVORITE HEARTLAND CEREAL GRAINS: WHEAT AND RYE.

1/2 teaspoon each fennel seed and salt

1/4 cup molasses

*3 tablespoons butter or margarine, at room temperature, cut
into 1/2-inch pieces*

1/3 cup boiling water

1/4 cup warm (105° to 115° F) water

1 tablespoon honey

1 package active dry yeast

3/4 cup warm (105° to 115° F) milk

1 cup rye flour

3 cups all-purpose flour

1/2 cup raisins or hulled sunflower seeds

Place fennel seed, salt, molasses, and butter in large bowl of electric mixer fitted with dough hook. Add boiling water, mix in, and let cool.

Meanwhile, in small bowl combine the warm water and honey. Dissolve yeast in mixture and let stand until bubbly, 5 to 10 minutes.

Stir yeast into cooled molasses mixture. Add milk and both flours, and knead 3 minutes. Gather dough together and turn out onto floured board. Knead in raisins until evenly distributed, 2 to 4 minutes. Form into ball, place in oiled bowl, and turn to oil top. Cover bowl lightly and let dough rise in warm, draft-free area until double in bulk, about 1 1/2 hours.

Punch dough down. Shape into loaf and place seam side down in oiled 5-by-9-by-3-inch loaf pan. Cover and let rise until double in bulk, about 1 hour.

Preheat oven to 375° F.

Bake until bread sounds hollow when tapped, 35 to 40 minutes. Remove bread from pan. Cool on wire rack.

DARK RYE BREAD

MAKES 1 LOAF

❋

SERVED WITH A VARIETY OF SAUSAGES, CHEESES, AND MUSTARDS, THIS MIDWESTERN VERSION OF A BLACK FOREST-STYLE BREAD CAN BE THE MAIN ATTRACTION OF A HEARTY HEARTLAND BUFFET SUPPER OR LUNCH. AN ELECTRIC MIXER WITH A DOUGH HOOK MAKES LIGHT WORK OF HEAVY DOUGHS SUCH AS THIS ONE.

1 package active dry yeast

1/3 cup warm (105° to 115° F) water

1/3 cup buttermilk

1 cup cold water, plus 1 tablespoon

1/4 cup dill or sour pickle juice

2 tablespoons vegetable shortening, melted

1 1/2 tablespoons sugar

1/2 teaspoon salt

1 tablespoon caraway seed

1 teaspoon dill seed

3 to 3 1/2 cups rye

1 cup whole-wheat flour

1 tablespoon water

1 egg yolk

In small bowl dissolve yeast in the warm water and let stand until bubbly, 5 to 10 minutes.

Meanwhile, heat buttermilk in saucepan over medium heat and pour into bowl of electric mixer fitted with dough hook. Stir in the 1 cup cold water, pickle juice, shortening, sugar, salt, and dill and caraway seeds. Stir in yeast mixture. Add rye and whole-wheat flours and beat in. Turn out onto lightly floured board and knead until smooth, about 3 minutes.

Form into ball, place in oiled bowl, and turn to oil top. Cover bowl lightly and let dough rise in warm, draft-free area until nearly doubled in bulk, about 1 1/2 hours.

Punch down dough. Turn out onto floured board and knead 1 minute. Shape into loaf and place in oiled 5-by-9-by-3-inch loaf pan. Cover lightly with towel and let rise in warm, draft-free area until doubled in bulk, about 1 hour.

Preheat oven to 375° F.

In small bowl mix together the 1 tablespoon water and egg yolk. Brush loaf with egg wash. Using a single-edge razor blade, make a slit down length of loaf.

Bake until bread sounds hollow when tapped, about 45 minutes. Remove from pan. Cool on wire rack.

HONEY, SUNFLOWER SEED, AND CRACKED-WHEAT LOAF

MAKES 4 SMALL LOAVES

❈

CRACKED-WHEAT CEREAL AND WHOLE-WHEAT FLOUR ARE AVAILABLE FROM NAUVOO MILL AND BAKING COMPANY, NAUVOO, ILLINOIS (SEE 236).

2 1/2 cups warm (105° to 115° F) water

2 tablespoons honey

2 tablespoons active dry yeast

1 tablespoon salt

1 tablespoon olive oil

1/2 cup cracked-wheat cereal, soaked in enough boiling water
    to measure 1 cup

3 cups stone-ground whole-wheat flour

3 to 5 cups unbleached flour

1 cup unsalted, roasted, hulled sunflower seeds

Proof the yeast in the half cup of warm water with the honey. When yeast foams, stir in remaining water, salt, oil, and cereal. Add the whole-wheat flour and three cups of the unbleached flour. Add the sunflower seeds and knead dough with an electric mixer. If dough is sticky, add more unbleached flour. When the dough is the proper consistency, it will clean the sides of the mixer bowl.

Place dough in a large bowl coated with olive oil and cover with a towel. Place in a warm spot and allow to rise until doubled in bulk, about 1 hour.

Turn dough out on a floured surface and pat out into a circle about 1-inch thick. Cut into 4 pieces and pinch the corners together to form a round loaf. Place loaves, pinched side down, on prepared cookie sheets. Cover. Allow to rise again for about 1 hour.

Preheat oven to 400° F. Slash tops of loaves. Bake for 30 minutes or until loaves sound hollow when tapped.

THREE-GRAIN BREAD

MAKES 1 LOAF

✳

WHOLE-WHEAT BREAD GETS AN EXTRA BOOST FROM MILLET AND BULGUR WHEAT, ADDING A NUTTY FLAVOR AND CRUNCHY TEXTURE TO THE NATURAL GOODNESS OF "THE RISEN LOAF." MILLET, BULGUR WHEAT, AND WHOLE-WHEAT FLOUR ARE AVAILABLE FROM SPECIAL-TY FOOD SHOPS AND NATURAL FOOD STORES, AS WELL AS SOME SUPERMARKETS.

1 cup warm (105° to 115° F) water
3 tablespoons honey
1 package active dry yeast
1/3 cup vegetable oil
1 1/2 cups whole-wheat flour
1/2 teaspoon salt
1 1/2 cups all-purpose flour
1/3 cup millet
1/3 cup bulgur wheat

In a small bowl combine the warm water and honey. Dissolve yeast in mixture and let stand until bubbly, 5 to 10 minutes.

Meanwhile, combine all remaining ingredients in large bowl of electric mixer fitted with dough hook. Add yeast mixture and beat in.

Form into ball, place in oiled bowl, and turn to oil top. Cover bowl and let dough rise in warm, draft-free area until double in size, about 1 1/2 hours.

Punch dough down. Turn out onto floured board and knead 2 minutes. Shape into loaf and place seam side down in oiled 5-by-9-by-3 inch loaf pan. Cover lightly with towel and let rise in warm, draft-free area until doubled in bulk, about 1 hour.

Meanwhile, preheat oven to 350° F.

Bake until bread sounds hollow when tapped, about 40 minutes. Remove from pan. Cool on wire rack.

MARZIPAN-FILLED PASTRIES

MAKES ABOUT 15 PASTRIES

❋

MADE FROM FINELY GROUND ALMONDS, SUGAR, AND EGG WHITES, ALMOND PASTE AND MARZI-
PAN HAVE BEEN USED IN CAKES AND PASTRIES FOR CENTURIES. BOTH ALMOND PASTE, WHICH IS
UNCOOKED, AND MARZIPAN, WHICH IS COOKED AND SOMEWHAT FIRMER, ARE AVAILABLE IN
GOURMET FOOD SHOPS AND SOME SUPERMARKETS.

3 1/2 to 4 cups flour

1 package active dry yeast

1/4 cup sugar

1/4 teaspoon salt

1 cup milk, at room temperature

1 1/4 cups (3 1/2 sticks) butter or margarine, cut into 1/2-inch
  pieces

1 egg

1 teaspoon vanilla extract

FOR FILLING:

1 1/2 cups almond paste

1/2 cup ground almonds

1 egg

2 tablespoons fresh orange juice

FOR ICING:

1 cup confectioner's sugar

3 tablespoons fresh orange juice

Sift flour into large bowl of electric mixer fitted with dough hook. Sprinkle with yeast and sugar. Add salt, milk, 1/4 cup of the butter, egg, and vanilla. Mix at low speed 1 minute, then at high speed 4 or 5 minutes. The dough should be smooth and pliable. Let rest 5 minutes. Alternatively, mix the ingredients with a wooden spoon.

Gather dough together and roll out on lightly floured board into an 8-by-15-inch rectangle. Put remaining butter pieces over half the dough. Fold other half of dough over butter-covered section. Press together lightly with rolling pin.

Roll out dough again to 8-by-15-inch rectangle. Fold both narrow sides over center. Then, starting from long side, fold in half, forming 4 layers. Wrap and refrigerate 15 minutes. Repeat rolling and folding. Wrap and refrigerate again 15 minutes.

Meanwhile, prepare filling by combining almond paste, almonds, egg, and juice in bowl. Stir until smooth.

Preheat oven to 400° F. Butter baking sheet.

Roll out dough to 12-by-15-inch rectangle. Spread filling over half of dough. Fold other half of dough over filled half. Press lightly with rolling pin. Cut dough in half lengthwise. Cut each half into 7 or 8 1-inch-wide strips. Twisting ends in opposite directions, form each strip into an *S* shape and arrange on prepared baking sheet. Let stand in warm area for 15 minutes.

Bake until golden brown, about 15 minutes.

While cookies are baking, make icing by combining sugar and orange juice in small mixing bowl and stirring until smooth.

Using spatula, carefully transfer pastries to wire rack to cool. Drizzle with icing while still warm.

FROSTED CINNAMON ROLLS

MAKES 12 LARGE ROLLS

✳

DRIZZLED WITH FROSTING AND STUDDED WITH RAISINS, THESE FIST-SIZED ROLLS ARE AN ALL-AMERICAN CLASSIC FOR SUNDAY BREAKFAST OR BRUNCH.

1 cup milk

1/4 cup (1/2 stick) butter or margarine, cut into 1/2-inch pieces

2 tablespoons plus 1 cup sugar

1 package active dry yeast

1/4 cup warm (105° to 115°F) water

2 eggs, lightly beaten

1/2 cup sour cream

3 cups flour

2 tablespoons ground cinnamon

1 1/2 cups raisins

FOR GLAZE:

6 ounces cream cheese, at room temperature, cut into 1/2-inch pieces

1/4 cup milk

1 cup sifted confectioner's sugar

1 teaspoon vanilla extract

In saucepan over medium heat, scald milk. Stir in butter and 2 tablespoons sugar and pour into large bowl of electric mixer. Cool to lukewarm.

In small bowl dissolve yeast in the warm water and let stand until bubbly, 5 to 10 minutes.

Add yeast mixture to milk mixture. Mix in eggs and sour cream, then slowly beat in flour. Turn out dough onto floured surface and knead until smooth, 2 to 5 minutes.

Form into ball, place in oiled bowl and turn to oil top. Cover bowl lightly and let dough rise in warm, draft-free area until doubled in bulk, about 1 1/2 hours.

Punch dough down and again gather into ball. Cover with foil and refrigerate at least

6 hours or as long as overnight. Remove from refrigerator 1/2 hour before rolling out.

Preheat oven to 375° F. Butter muffin pan(s). On lightly floured board roll out dough into 6-by-12-inch rectangle. In bowl mix together 1 cup sugar, cinnamon, and raisins. Sprinkle mixture over dough. Starting from long side, roll up dough jelly-roll style. Cut roll crosswise in 2-inch slices. Arrange each slice cut side down in prepared pan. Let rise in warm, draft-free area until nearly doubled, about 40 minutes.

Bake until golden brown, about 20 minutes.

While rolls are baking, prepare glaze. In bowl beat cream cheese until smooth. Beat in milk, sugar, and vanilla.

Invert rolls onto wire rack and cool 5 minutes. Drizzle glaze over rolls. Cool completely before serving.

FRIED BISCUITS WITH APPLE BUTTER

MAKES 10 TO 12 BISCUITS

❈

NASHVILLE HOUSE IN NASHVILLE, INDIANA, IS FAMOUS FOR ITS FRIED BISCUITS, BROUGHT TO THE TABLE PIPING HOT WITH APPLE BUTTER.

1/4 cup warm (105° to 115° F) water
1/2 teaspoon honey
1 package active dry yeast
3 to 3 1/2 cups flour
1/2 teaspoon salt
1 cup milk
5 tablespoons vegetable shortening, cut into 1/2-inch pieces
3 cups vegetable oil
Apple butter (see page 172)

In small bowl combine the warm water and honey. Dissolve yeast mixture and let stand until bubbly, 5 to 10 minutes.

Meanwhile, in large bowl of electric mixer fitted with dough hook, stir together flour and salt. In saucepan over medium heat, combine milk and shortening and scald. Cool to lukewarm. Add milk and yeast mixture to flour and mix in, then beat until dough forms, about 4 minutes. Dough will be sticky. Turn onto floured board and knead until smooth, about 2 minutes. Form into ball, place in oiled bowl, and turn to oil top. Cover bowl lightly and let dough rise in warm, draft-free area until doubled in bulk, about 1 1/2 hours.

Punch down dough. On lightly floured board roll out dough 1/2 to 3/4 inch thick. Using 2 1/2- or 3-inch cookie cutter, cut out rounds.

In deep pan heat oil to 360° to 370° F; slide 4 to 6 rolls into it. Fry, turning with slotted spoon after 3 minutes, until golden brown on both sides, about 5 to 6 minutes total cooking time. Remove to paper towels to drain briefly.

Place rolls in bread dish. Bring to table piping hot with Apple Butter (see page 172).

TRADITIONAL CORNBREAD

MAKES 16 SQUARES OR 8 LARGE WEDGES

❋

WHITE CORNMEAL OR YELLOW FOR CORNBREAD? WHOLE MILK OR BUTTERMILK? THE ANSWERS VARY WITH THE COOK AND THE REGION, AND ALL THE ALTERNATIVES ARE ALMOST EQUALLY TASTY. WHITE AND YELLOW CORNMEAL ARE SIMILAR IN TASTE. BUTTERMILK, HOWEVER, WINS HANDS DOWN, PROVIDING BOTH A TANGY FLAVOR AND A YEASTY ELEMENT TO LIGHTEN THE BREAD. TRY THIS RECIPE IN CORNBREAD DRESSING (SEE PAGE 112).

Butter, for greasing pan
1 cup cornmeal
1 cup flour
3 tablespoons sugar
4 teaspoons baking powder
1/2 teaspoon salt
1/3 cup butter or shortening at room temperature
1 egg
1 cup buttermilk

Preheat oven to 400° F. Grease a 10-inch cast-iron skillet (or an 8-by-8-inch baking pan) and place in oven to heat.

In a large bowl stir together cornmeal, flour, sugar, baking powder, and salt. Use a pastry blender, two knives, or fingers to cut in butter or shortening to make a coarse but even meal.

In a medium bowl beat together egg and buttermilk and pour into cornmeal mixture. Stir strongly but briefly, scooping from the bottom, just until thoroughly blended.

Pour mixture into heated baking pan. Bake for about 25 minutes, until top is lightly browned and corn bread shrinks from the sides of the pan. Serve warm.

WISCONSIN BEER BREAD WITH FENNEL SEEDS

MAKES 1 LOAF

❋

FLAVORED WITH FENNEL AND CELERY SEEDS, THIS UNUSUAL BREAD IS QUICK AND EASY TO MAKE. THE BEER SHOULD BE AT ROOM TEMPERATURE.

Preheat oven to 350° F.

In large bowl of electric mixer, combine flour, sugar, beer, and fennel seed. Beat until well blended. Pour batter into oiled 5-by-9-by-3 inch loaf pan. Sprinkle with celery seeds.

3 cups self-rising flour

1/3 cup sugar

1 can (12 oz) light beer

1 teaspoon fennel seed

1/4 teaspoon celery seed

Bake until tester inserted in bread comes out dry, about 1 hour. Cool on wire rack. Serve warm.

BEER

As aficionados of "Laverne and Shirley" can attest, beer built Milwaukee. Wisconsin outdoes its neighbors in sheer numbers, with more breweries per capita than any other state. But many breweries throughout the Midwest (the Heartland is now home to more than one hundred breweries) have practiced their art for over a century, capitalizing on the abundance of locally grown cereal grains. Beer, not wine, was the drink of choice for numerous Midwest settlers, especially those hailing from Germany, Poland, England, and Ireland. The burgeoning beer industry proved profitable for early brewmaster-entrepreneurs. Several local cities have a mansion-lined boulevard, nicknamed "beer barons' row" and the names of the beer barons are household words.

Green Tomato Bread

MAKES 1 LOAF

✱

AN EARLY FROST SIGNALS THE END OF SUMMER'S BOUNTY OF RED RIPE TOMATOES. THRIFTY MIDWESTERN GARDENERS AND COOKS HAVE MANY WAYS TO PUT UNRIPENED TOMATOES TO GOOD USE, INCLUDING THIS WHOLESOME LOAF.

1/4 cup (1/2 stick) butter, at room temperature

3/4 cup sugar

1 egg

1/2 teaspoon salt

1/4 teaspoon ground ginger

1 teaspoon vanilla extract

1 cup green tomato purée

1 3/4 cups flour

1 1/4 teaspoons baking soda

1/2 teaspoon baking powder

1/4 cup plain yogurt

1/2 cup golden raisins

1/2 cup chopped walnuts

Preheat oven to 350° F. Grease 5-by-9-by-3-inch loaf pan.

In large bowl of electric mixer, beat together butter and sugar until light. Beat in egg, salt, ginger, vanilla, and green tomato purée. (Cut 2 or 3 green tomatoes into large chunks and purée in food processor.) Then beat in flour, baking soda, baking powder, and yogurt until just mixed. Stir in raisins and walnuts. Do not overbeat.

Pour batter into prepared pan. Bake until golden brown and until tester inserted in center comes out dry, about 40 minutes. Cool on wire rack.

FUNNEL CAKES

MAKES 18 CAKES

✳

NAMED FOR THE FAMILIAR KITCHEN UTENSIL USED IN THE PREPARATION OF THIS UNUSUAL SPICED CAKE, FUNNEL CAKES ARE DELICIOUS SERVED WITH CRUSHED STRAWBERRIES AND SWEET-ENED WHIPPED CREAM.

2 eggs

3 tablespoons plain yogurt

1 3/4 cups milk

3 cups flour, sifted

1/2 teaspoon baking soda

1/2 teaspoon ground cinnamon

1/4 teaspoon salt

1/4 teaspoon ground nutmeg

canola oil, for frying

Confectioner's sugar

In deep mixing bowl beat eggs until light and fluffy. Stir in yogurt and milk until well mixed, then stir in flour, baking soda, cinnamon, salt, and nutmeg. Batter should be thin.

In deep sauté or similar pan, pour in oil to depth of 1 inch, and heat to 375° F. Transfer batter to pitcher for easy handling. With your finger over tip of funnel with 1/2-inch hole, fill top of funnel with batter.

Position funnel over hot oil and remove finger from tip of funnel. Let batter gently fall into oil, forming concentric circles. Make 3 cakes at a time. Fry until golden brown on first side, about 2 minutes. Using spatula and fork turn cakes over and continue cooking until golden brown on second side, about 30 seconds longer.

Using slotted spoon, remove to paper towels to drain briefly. Sprinkle with confectioner's sugar. Serve hot.

GIANT BUTTERMILK APPLE MUFFINS

MAKES 6 LARGE MUFFINS

❀

THESE ARE DELIGHTFUL ADDITIONS TO ALMOST ANY MEAL—BREAKFAST, BRUNCH, LUNCH, OR FAMILY SUPPERS.

To make streusel topping, place butter, flour, cinnamon, and sugars in bowl and cut in butter until coarse and crumbly. Set aside.

Preheat oven to 400° F. Grease 6-hole oversized muffin pan with butter.

In bowl toss together apples, 1/3 cup of the sugar and 1/4 cup of the flour. Set aside.

1 to 2 tablespoons butter or margarine

2 or 3 large cooking apples, peeled, cored, and chopped (3 cups)

2/3 cup sugar

2 cups flour

1 3/4 teaspoons baking powder

1/2 teaspoon baking soda

1/3 teaspoon salt

1/2 cup buttermilk

2 eggs, lightly beaten

1/2 teaspoon ground cinnamon

FOR STREUSEL TOPPING:

3 tablespoons unsalted butter or margarine, at room temperature

3 tablespoons flour

3/4 cup granulated sugar

1/4 cup firmly packed light brown sugar

1/2 teaspoon ground cinnamon

In large mixing bowl, combine remaining 1 3/4 cups flour, baking powder, baking soda, and salt. Stir in buttermilk, eggs, and cinnamon until mixed; do not overbeat. Batter may be lumpy. Stir in apple mixture.

Ladle batter into muffin pan, filling half full. Sprinkle streusel topping evenly over muffins.

Bake until golden brown, 20 to 25 minutes. Cool 5 to 10 minutes, then remove from pan.

THE HARVEST DINNER

Throughout the Heartland states, harvest day is a tradition that carries a significance to match that of a major American holiday. From the middle of the nineteenth century to the present, the late summer or fall harvest has been an occasion for both a joyful social celebration and serious reflection on the importance of a bountiful yield.

The threshing ring, a cooperative system that emerged during the last century, was made up of neighboring farmers and hired laborers who rotated from farm to farm to assist in the exhausting but rewarding work of harvest. The shared use of machinery and the trading off of labor afforded individual farmers convenience, economy, and camaraderie.

The farm wives joined in the prodigious harvest effort by creating what came to be the high point of the season, the harvest dinner. From before dawn, the farm kitchen was an explosion of activity, directed and organized as efficiently and tightly as the precision movements of an army in the field.

When the hot, tired, sweaty harvesters sat down at the table, they were greeted by a cornucopia of Heartland abundance: fruit and vegetable salads, relishes and pickles, hot breads and baking powder biscuits, roast beef and pork, slices of fresh red tomatoes and fried green tomatoes, onions and cucumbers in vinegar and oil, steaming piles of buttered corn on the cob, baked beans, fresh green beans and bacon, glazed sweet potatoes, jams, jellies, cookies, freshly baked fruit and cream pies, muffins, cakes, and pitchers of iced tea and pots of hot coffee.

Reflecting on just such a harvest-day dinner, it is hard to believe that the harvesters were able to do even a lick of work until long after they rose from the table.

PLUMP BLUEBERRY MUFFINS

MAKES 9 MUFFINS

✳

A GENTLE TOUCH ASSURES YOU OF LIGHT, TENDER MUFFINS—MIX THE BATTER JUST ENOUGH TO MOISTEN THE DRY INGREDIENTS. STIR IN THE BLUEBERRIES WITH THE LAST FEW STROKES.

2 cups flour

1/3 cup sugar

1 tablespoon baking powder

1/2 teaspoon salt

1/4 teaspoon ground nutmeg

1 egg

1 cup milk

3 tablespoons butter or margarine (melted and cooled) or salad oil

1/2 teaspoon grated lemon rind

1 cup blueberries

2 tablespoons sugar mixed with 1/8 teaspoon cinnamon

Grease 2 3/4-inch muffin pan. Pre-heat oven to 400° F.

In a large bowl stir together flour, the 1/3 cup sugar, baking powder, salt, and nutmeg.

In a medium bowl beat egg with milk, butter, and lemon rind. Add egg mixture to flour mixture, stirring just until dry ingredients are moistened. Stir in blueberries with fewest possible strokes.

Fill prepared pans about three-fourths full. Sprinkle tops lightly with sugar-cinnamon mixture.

Bake until barely browned (about 30 minutes). Serve warm.

CHAPTER 6

From the Waters
of the Midwest

Good fishing is a way of life in and around the inland lakes and rivers of the prairie states. The Chicago Fish House, one of the nation's top fish and shellfish wholesalers, buys and sells 100 tons of fish weekly from all over the world. With so many fish to choose from, Midwesterners  can enjoy fish every week for a year without repeating varieties. A second- and third-generation business run by the Mitsakopoulos family, the company receives daily shipments from across the United States, Europe, South America, New Zealand, and Australia.

BRAISED SWEET-AND-SOUR CATFISH

SERVES 4

❋

THE JUBILEE ON THE BOARDWALK IS THE FIRST FLOATING RESTAURANT IN THE QUAD CITIES (MOLINE AND ROCK ISLAND, ILLINOIS, AND DAVENPORT AND BETTENDORF, IOWA). OWNER-DEVELOPER JOE SCHADLER HAS TRANSFORMED A ONCE-DRAB INDUSTRIAL AREA OF MOLINE INTO A FESTIVAL ON A MISSISSIPPI RIVER BARGE. THE FOLLOWING JUBILEE RECIPE FOR MISSISSIPPI CATFISH IS FROM CHEF KAZUHIRA HISHIDA.

Season catfish with salt and pepper, then dredge in cornstarch to coat completely. In deep sauté pan pour in oil to depth of 2 to 3 inches and heat to 350° F. Working in batches fry catfish until cooked through, golden, and crispy. Using slotted spatula remove to paper towels to drain.

To make sauce, in bowl stir together all ingredients,

4 catfish (8 oz each), cleaned

Salt and pepper, to taste

2 cups cornstarch

Peanut oil, for deep-frying

FOR SWEET-AND-SOUR SAUCE:

1/2 cup each bottled teriyaki sauce, rice vinegar, water, honey, and ketchup

1 tablespoon cornstarch

Dash cayenne pepper

FOR VEGETABLES:

2 tablespoons sesame oil

1 teaspoon chopped garlic

1 teaspoon chopped or julienned fresh ginger

1 carrot, peeled and julienned

2 celery stalks, julienned

1 zucchini, julienned

16 ears baby corn

4 water chestnuts, sliced

2 tablespoons sesame seed

mixing well. Set aside.

To cook vegetables, in skillet over medium heat, heat sesame oil. Add garlic and ginger and sauté until translucent, 1 or 2 minutes; do not brown. Place fish in skillet and add sauce, carrot, celery, zucchini, corn, and water chestnuts. Cook until sauce reduces and is absorbed by fish, and vegetables cook slightly, just a few minutes.

Place fish on serving platter and arrange vegetables decoratively around them. Pour sauce over all and sprinkle with sesame seed. Serve immediately.

CANADIAN WALLEYE PIKE WITH MUSTARD AND DILL SAUCE

SERVES 2

❋

PIKE OFTEN APPEARS ON JEWISH HOLIDAY MENUS IN THE FORM OF GEFILTE FISH (FISH DUMPLINGS). THIS RECIPE FOR CANADIAN WALLEYE FEATURES A RICH CREAM SAUCE MADE TANGY WITH MUSTARD AND COLORFUL WITH FRESH DILL.

To make sauce, in saucepan bring wine and stock to boil. Reduce heat to medium and simmer until reduced to 3/4 cup. Add mustard and cream, stir well, and remove from heat. Whisk in egg yolks, one at a time. Whisk in butter. Strain sauce and then add dill and salt and pepper. Keep warm over low heat.

FOR MUSTARD-DILL SAUCE:

1/2 cup dry white wine

1 cup fish stock

3 tablespoons whole-grain mustard

1/4 cup whipping cream

3 egg yolks

2 tablespoons unsalted butter

1 tablespoon minced fresh dill

Salt and pepper, to taste

FOR FISH:

1 Canadian walleye pike (8 to 10 oz), cleaned

1 egg

1/2 cup fresh bread crumbs

2 tablespoons butter

FOR GARNISH:

2 cucumbers, peeled, seeded, and sliced

1/2 red onion, thinly sliced

1/4 cup rice wine vinegar

Salt and pepper, to taste

To prepare fish, beat egg in shallow dish. Place bread crumbs in separate shallow bowl. Coat fish first with egg and then with crumbs. In skillet over medium heat, melt butter. Add fish and sauté, turning once, until golden brown on both sides and fish flakes easily when tested with knife point, 3 to 4 minutes.

While fish is cooking, in bowl toss together all garnish ingredients and spread out on serving platter. Place fish atop garnish and serve with sauce.

SMELT

For many midwesterners smelting is their initiation into the joys of fishing—without hooks, without bait, without blood. When the smelt are running in Lake Michigan, all it takes are a net and a boat to capture enough silvery, squirmy smelt to feed an army.

Such expeditions take place in the middle of the night in early spring, so there's still quite a chill in the air along the Lake Michigan shoreline. Hundreds of people bundled in scarves and parkas, long underwear and sweaters, boots, and blankets huddle together around cookstoves, lanterns glowing. They are laughing, joking, swapping fish stories and advice, arguing good-naturedly over equipment and methods, waiting, waiting, in the cold night air for that magic moment when the water becomes alive with thousands of smelt and the season officially opens.

These hardy souls come from every walk of life. What unites them during the four-week season is their passion for this event. There is no limit to the catch. On a "good run," it's possible to walk away with hundreds of the little three-to-seven-inch fish as they move toward shore to spawn.

If you have pressing engagements, don't encourage any of the anglers to discuss their recipes for these sweet morsels. Deep-fry advocates are probably in the majority, but there is a vocal group that insists on panfrying right there on the dock. As the evening progresses the frantic cleaning begins. The fish must be cleaned immediately and eaten on the spot, or placed with water in a milk carton and frozen for later use.

In the best midwestern tradition, fried smelt are always accompanied by cold beer, heated French bread, and a spicy dipping sauce.

CHICAGO-STYLE PAN-FRIED SMELT

SERVES 6

✳

PARTISANS OF PAN-FRIED SMELT PREPARE THEM THIS WAY: SNIP OFF HEAD WITH SCISSORS AND SLIT BELLY OPEN. USE ROUNDED SPOON OR FINGERS TO REMOVE INNARDS. YOU MAY SNIP OFF BACK FIN AND TAIL IF SMELT IS LARGE. SMELT ARE TRADITION-ALLY SERVED WITH COLD BEER AND HOT FRENCH BREAD.

FOR HORSERADISH SAUCE:
1 1/2 cups bottled chili sauce
2 tablespoons well-drained bottled horseradish, or to taste

2 pounds smelt, cleaned
1 can (12 oz) beer

1 cup flour
1/2 teaspoon salt
1/4 teaspoon each black pepper and cayenne pepper
1/8 teaspoon garlic powder
1/2 cup (1 stick) butter or margarine, (or equal parts each butter and margarine)
Lemon wedges

To make sauce, in small bowl stir together chili sauce and horseradish. Cover light-ly and refrigerate.

Place smelt in self-sealing plastic bag. Pour beer over smelt and seal top securely. Let stand at room temperature 1 hour.

In another plastic bag mix together flour, salt, black pepper, cayenne pepper, and garlic powder. Remove smelt from beer, shake each lightly to remove excess liquid, and roll in flour mixture.

In large, heavy-bottomed skillet, over medium-high heat melt butter and heat until bubbly. Add smelt and fry, turning once, until golden brown.

Transfer to serving platter and bring to table. Serve with sauce and lemon wedges.

GRILLED DOVER SOLE, RED SHRIMP, TARRAGON BEURRE BLANC, AND DEEP-FRIED SPINACH

SERVES 4

❋

CHEF CAROLYN BUSTER (SEE PAGE 228) CREATED THIS TANTALIZING BLEND OF FLAVORS, COLORS, AND TEXTURES FROM LOCAL PRODUCE AND FRESH INGREDIENTS FLOWN IN DAILY TO THE HEARTLAND FROM ALL OVER THE WORLD.

Preheat oven to 450° F or preheat grill.

To make sauce, in saucepan over medium heat, melt 1/4 cup of the butter. Add shallots and sauté until translucent; do not brown. Add tarragon vinegar and white wine and reduce over high heat to about 1/2 cup liquid or less. Cut remaining butter in small pieces and whisk into sauce, piece by piece. Whisk in mustard and white pepper and remove from heat. In bowl placed over simmering water, whisk egg yolks. Slowly whisk in butter sauce.

Grill shrimp and sole (skin side down) on greased grill rack, or place skin side up on

FOR TARRAGON BEURRE BLANC:

3 large shallots, minced

2 cups (1 pound) butter, divided

6 tablespoons tarragon vinegar

2 cups dry white wine

3 tablespoons Dijon-style mustard (preferably Grey Poupon), or to taste

White pepper, to taste

2 egg yolks

8 Spanish shrimp, peeled and deveined

2 1/2 pounds Dover sole

Butter and salt, if baking

1 pound spinach, trimmed, washed and thoroughly dried

Vegetable oil, for deep-frying

sheet of aluminum foil and top with small piece of butter and sprinkling of salt. Cooking time will depend upon thickness of fish. Flesh should be opaque and firm to the touch.

In deep sauté pan pour in oil to depth of 2 inches and heat to 375° F. Carefully slide spinach leaves into hot oil, a few at a time. Leaves will immediately turn brilliant green and become crisp. Remove to paper towels to drain. Repeat until all are fried.

To serve arrange spinach on individual plates. Place fish topped with shrimp on spinach. Drizzle with sauce and serve hot.

SMOKED STURGEON WITH GREEN PEPPERCORNS

SERVES 6

❋

THE PUNGENCY OF THE GREEN PEPPERCORNS IN THIS DISH BALANCES THE RICHNESS OF THE STURGEON. OILY FISH SUCH AS STURGEON ARE IDEAL FOR SMOKING.

Arrange sturgeon steaks on tray. Mix together green and black peppercorns and pat firmly into both sides of sturgeon steaks.

Prepare smoker according to manufacturer's instructions. Fill coal pan two-thirds full with charcoal. Heat coals until hot and ashen. Sprinkle coals with hickory chips. Fill water pan with hot water.

6 sturgeon steaks (6 to 7 oz each)

2 tablespoons green peppercorns, coarsely cracked

1 tablespoon black peppercorns, coarsely cracked

2 cups hickory, cherry, or other aromatic woodchips, soaked 30 minutes in water to cover and drained

Place sturgeon steaks on top rack of smoker. Cover and smoke 30 to 45 minutes. Check doneness after 30 minutes; fish is done when flesh is firm to touch.

Arrange on platter and serve warm or cold.

GLACIER SPRINGS TROUT WITH DUXELLES

SERVES 6

✳

SINCE 1972, THE ROWE INN IN ELLSWORTH, MICHIGAN, HAS BEEN OWNED AND OPERATED BY ALBERT "WES" AND ARLENE WESTHOVEN. LOCALLY GROWN PRODUCTS ARE FEATURED ON AN EVER-CHANGING MENU, REFLECTING THE SEASONS AND THE BOUNTY OF THE NORTH WOODS. THE ROWE INN'S CHEF KATHLEEN RUSS GREW UP ON A FARM IN NORTHERN MICHIGAN "EATING REAL GOOD FOOD."

IN THIS RECIPE, YOU CAN USE ALL BUTTON MUSHROOMS. BETTER, HOWEVER, TO USE AT LEAST HALF WILD MUSHROOMS (CÈPES AND/OR MORELS) AND HALF BUTTON MUSHROOMS. IF USING DRIED WILD MUSHROOMS, RECONSTITUTE THEM IN WARM WATER AND SAVE THE SOAKING LIQUID, BUT STRAIN IT TWICE THROUGH FILTER PAPER BEFORE USING.

FOR DUXELLES:

6 tablespoons (3/4 stick) unsalted butter

3/4 cup very finely chopped onion

1 pound fresh mushrooms, very finely chopped (see introduction)

1/4 cup finely chopped shallots

1/2 teaspoon each ground ginger, salt, and pepper

1/4 cup Madeira

2 tablespoons brandy

6 rainbow trout (about 8 oz each), cleaned and boned

Melted butter or margarine

Salt and pepper, to taste

Fine dry bread crumbs

Pickled Leeks (see page 169)

To make duxelles, in skillet over medium heat, melt butter. Add onion and sauté until golden, 5 to 8 minutes. Add mushrooms, shallot, ginger, salt, and pepper. Continue to sauté over medium heat until all moisture evaporates, or a couple minutes. Add wine, brandy, and mushroom soaking liquid (if using).

Continue cooking until liquid has evaporated, a few minutes longer. Cool completely.

Preheat oven to 375° F.

Brush insides of trout with melted butter and sprinkle with salt and pepper. Spread about 3 tablespoons mushroom mixture across each bottom fillet. Close fish, butter top, and sprinkle with bread crumbs. Generously butter baking sheet and sprinkle with bread crumbs. Arrange stuffed trout on sheet.

Bake until fish flakes easily when tested with knife point, 12 to 15 minutes. Serve with Pickled Leeks (see page 169).

HEARTLAND CAVIAR

There has always been a certain barrier between fine caviar and its lovers, namely cost. Quality caviar—traditionally, sturgeon roe—has been so expensive for so long that many people have been forced to compromise with lumpfish caviar, which is a sad imitation of what caviar should be. However, there is now relief: The Heartland produces several good varieties and the regional specialty—the golden caviar of Great Lakes whitefish—is probably the best value of any caviar currently available, with remarkable quality for a reasonable price.

Heartland Food Society member Carolyn Collins is founding director of Collins Caviar Company, based in Crystal Lake, Illinois, which produces much of the caviar the world is taking such an interest in. Using typical Heartland initiative, she has transformed her hobby of sports fishing and preparing fish roe into an international concern. "In the Chicago area there was access to everything needed to become a caviar producer," she notes with pleasure. Joining the whitefish roe is that from trout, salmon, sturgeon, and other fish found in the local waters.

To enjoy the Heartland's very special caviar harvest, spread it on warm buttered toast points and drizzle with lemon juice. Serve crepes or little boiled potatoes with sour cream and caviar. Sprinkle a little on raw oysters for a decadent treat. Or dazzle your guests: Fill miniature cream puffs with sour cream, caviar, and chopped chives. You can use your imagination—and use it often—with the wonderful caviar the Heartland is making available to one and all.

GREAT LAKES WHITEFISH WITH BASIL CREAM SAUCE AND GOLDEN WHITEFISH ROE

SERVES 4

❋

AT HER L'ETOILE RESTAURANT IN MADISON, OWNER ODESSA PIPER RELIES ON THE FRESH SEA-SONAL PRODUCE OF WISCONSIN FARMERS. CO-CHEF ERIC RUPERT, WHO DEVELOPED THIS RECIPE, COMBINES TRADITIONAL COOKING TECHNIQUES WITH A STRAIGHTFORWARD, UNPRE-TENTIOUS APPROACH TO RECIPE DEVELOPMENT, AS DEMONSTRATED IN THIS DISH OF WHITEFISH FILLETS AND ROE (FISH EGGS—ALSO A HEARTLAND SPECIAL-TY—SEE PAGE 100) WITH A BASIL-FLAVORED CREAM SAUCE.

2 cups white wine

1 cup basil vinegar

1/3 cup chopped shallot

2 cups whipping cream

1/2 teaspoon dried basil

Salt and pepper, to taste

4 whitefish portions (6 oz each)

Melted butter or margarine, to brush on fish

1/4 cup chopped fresh basil

2 ounces golden whitefish roe (caviar)

Preheat oven to 400° F.

In heavy, nonreactive saucepan combine wine, vinegar, and shallot. Place over high heat and reduce until liquid is almost totally evaporated. Add cream and reduce heat. Add dried basil and reduce until cream thickens slightly to sauce consistency. Add salt and pepper. Strain into small bowl. Set bowl in a larger bowl filled with warm water to keep warm until serving.

Arrange fish portions on greased baking sheet. Brush with butter and sprinkle with salt and pepper. Bake until fish flakes easily when tested with knife point, about 10 minutes.

Spoon sauce onto individual plates. Place fish on top of sauce. Sprinkle with fresh basil. Spoon 1/2 ounce caviar atop each serving. (Or stir caviar into sauce before spoon-ing onto plates.) Serve immediately.

PLANKED WHITEFISH
WITH GARLIC MASHED POTATOES

SERVES 4

❀

ASK YOUR FISHMONGER TO
CLEAN THE WHITEFISH, REMOVE
THE HEAD, AND THEN BUTTER-
FLY AND BONE THE FISH.

*Thin plank of hardwood, slightly larger than fish, soaked in
water to cover overnight and drained*

1 whitefish, salmon, or carp (2 1/2 pound)

2 tablespoons corn oil

2 tablespoons butter, melted

1/4 teaspoon salt

1/4 teaspoon white pepper

2 tablespoons fresh lemon or lime juice

Garlic Mashed Potatoes (see page 103)

1 lemon, cut into wedges

1/4 cup parsley sprigs for garnish

Place hardwood plank in cold oven and set oven to 450° F. (If plank is not available, use ovenproof metal tray.) After 10 minutes remove plank. Rub top of plank with oil and place fish, skin side down, in center. Brush fish with half of butter and sprinkle with salt, pepper, and lemon juice. Reduce oven temperature to 400° F.

Return plank to oven. Bake 12 to 14 minutes, brushing fish with remaining butter after 7 minutes. Test fish; if it does not flake easily when prodded with knife tip, reduce heat to 350° F and bake 5 minutes longer.

Preheat broiler.

Using pastry bag pipe garlic mashed potatoes around fish. Place plank under broiler and broil until potatoes brown on top, 3 to 4 minutes or less.

Garnish fish with lemon wedges and parsley sprigs and bring to table on plank.

GARLIC MASHED POTATOES

SERVES 6

✽

TO MAKE QUICK WORK OF MASHING POTATOES AND TO ELIMINATE LUMPS, USE AN OLD-FASHIONED POTATO RICER.

2 pounds potatoes, peeled and cut into quarters

1 teaspoon salt

3 tablespoons butter or margarine, or a mixture

1/4 teaspoon white pepper

1/2 cup milk or whipping cream or a mixture

3 cloves garlic (or more), crushed in press

In saucepan combine potatoes, salt, and water to cover. Bring to boil and boil until tender when pierced with fork, about 20 minutes. Drain well.

Pass potatoes through ricer into large bowl or place in bowl and mash with potato masher. Vigorously stir in butter, pepper, milk, and cream, and mashed garlic cloves until well blended. Pipe onto plank or place in warm serving dish.

DOOR COUNTY FISH BOIL

SERVES 12

❋

WISCONSIN NATIVES PRACTICE THE ART OF THE FISH BOIL. THIS SUMMERTIME FEAST IS A SPECIALTY OF THE WHITE GULL INN IN DOOR COUNTY. MANAGER LAUREL DUFFIN SAYS, "THE FISH BOIL, A DOOR COUNTY TRADITION, CAME VIA THE SCANDINAVIANS AS A MEANS OF FEEDING A LOT OF PEOPLE. NOW THOUSANDS OF TOURISTS EACH YEAR COME TO DOOR COUNTY TO SEE THE SHOW AND ENJOY THE FOOD."

TRADITIONAL ACCOMPANIMENTS INCLUDE COLE SLAW, LIMPA BREAD (SEE PAGE 71), LEMON WEDGES, ORANGE-DATE-NUT BREAD, PUMPKIN BREAD, AND CHERRY PIE (SEE PAGE 186).

At White Gull Inn, the fish is cooked outside over a wood fire, using a 22-gallon pot and two nets, one for the fish and one for the potatoes. This recipe is for cooking at

12 small red potatoes, unpeeled

8 quarts water

2 cups salt

12 whitefish steaks, (2 in. thick)

Melted butter

Lemon wedges

home on a kitchen stove. You will need a large pot (5-gallon capacity is ideal), preferably with removable basket or net for draining. For smaller quantities, a single basket or net is sufficient for both potatoes and fish. If your pot does not have a removable basket for draining, make a cheesecloth bag to hold the potatoes and one to hold the fish, or drain over the sink, in a colander.

The amount of salt used here is based on the amount of water. To expand this recipe, add 1 cup salt for each additional gallon water.

Pour the water into pot to boil; keep it boiling as much as possible throughout the cooking.

Cut a small slice from end of each potato, for flavor penetration. Add potatoes and half the salt to boiling water and cook 20 minutes. Test potatoes with a fork; they should be almost done.

Add whitefish with the remaining salt. Cook until fish are still firm but begin to pull away from the bone when lifted with a fork, 8 to 10 minutes.

At the inn, when cooking outside, a small amount of kerosene is tossed on the fire when fish is done, which causes the fish oils on the water's surface to boil over the sides of the pot. Do not attempt this on your stove at home; simply skim the oils off with a spoon while fish is cooking.

Lift cooked potatoes and fish from the water; drain. Serve immediately with melted butter and lemon.

WISCONSIN FISH FRY

SERVES 4

❋

THE LATE NANCY ABRAMS OF THE CHICAGO FISH HOUSE SAID IT SO WELL: "THE BOUNTY OF OUR MIDWEST STREAMS, LAKES, AND RIVERS IS LIKE A CORNUCOPIA OF FISH. FROM THE LEGENDARY MUSKIE TO COHO SALMON, THEY ARE THE STUFF OF SPORT FISHERMEN'S DREAMS. THE WHITEFISH, WALLEYED PIKE, LAKE PERCH, BASS (AND MUCH MORE) BRING TO OUR DINNER TABLE A FEAST OF KINGS."

ONE WAY WISCONSIN COOKS SHOW THEIR APPRECIATION FOR THE BOUNTY ABRAMS REFERRED TO IS THE TRADITION OF THE FISH FRY. THE BEER IN THE BATTER CREATES A FERMENTATION THAT HELPS ENSURE A DELICIOUSLY CRISP CRUST THAT DOES NOT ABSORB EXCESS OIL DURING FRYING.

1 1/2 cups all-purpose flour

1/2 teaspoon salt, plus salt for sprinkling on fish

1/4 teaspoon dried dill

1/8 teaspoon freshly ground pepper, plus pepper for sprinkling on fish

2 eggs, separated

1 tablespoon butter or margarine, melted

1 cup beer

3 cups peanut oil

1 1/2 pounds fish fillets such as lake perch, walleyed pike, northern pike, or crappie

Preheat oven to 250° F.

In large bowl stir together flour, 1/2 teaspoon salt, dill, and 1/8 teaspoon pepper. Make well in center and add egg yolks and butter to it. Add beer and stir to incorporate ingredients. Set aside for 3 minutes.

Meanwhile, in large heavy saucepan or deep-fryer, pour in oil and heat to 375° F. Place egg whites in deep bowl and beat until stiff peaks form. Pat fish fillets dry. Sprinkle fish with salt and pepper. Fold egg whites into batter. Coat fish with batter, shaking off excess.

Working in batches, carefully slip fish into hot oil. Fry, turning once, until golden on both sides, about 3 minutes. Using slotted spatula remove to paper towels to drain briefly. If necessary, keep warm on baking sheet in single layer in 250° F oven until all fish is cooked. (Do not keep too long in oven or batter will become soggy.)

Serve piping hot.

CARTHUSIAN GRILLED SALMON

SERVES 4

❋

OWNER PATRICIA POOLEY STARTED THE MOVEABLE FEAST IN 1977 AS A CATERING COMPANY, IN ANN ARBOR, MICHIGAN. THE BUSINESS HAS EXPANDED TO INCLUDE A RETAIL STORE IN NEARBY CHELSEA, A WHOLESALE BAKERY, AND A RESTAURANT, WHERE CHEF ANDREW KILE SERVES FRENCH-ACCENTED AMERICAN AND REGIONAL SPECIALTIES. THE RESTAURANT IS IN ANN ARBOR'S OLD WEST SIDE HISTORICAL DISTRICT.

4 salmon steaks (7 oz each)

Olive oil, to brush on salmon

2 tablespoons clarified butter

6 oz lobster meat

8 shrimp, peeled and deveined

1 tablespoon chopped garlic

1/2 cup fish stock

1/2 cup Chartreuse

1 cup whipping cream

Salt and pepper, to taste

1 teaspoon each chopped fresh basil, tarragon, and rosemary

1 pound French beans, trimmed and lightly steamed

Ready fire in charcoal grill. Brush salmon lightly with oil. Place on greased grill rack and grill, turning once, until fish flakes, about 7 minutes on each side. Do not overcook.

While salmon is grilling, prepare sauce. In sauté pan over medium heat, melt butter. Add lobster and shrimp and sauté until seafood is half done, a couple of minutes. Add garlic and sauté a second or so more; do not brown garlic. Pour in stock and Chartreuse and deglaze pan. Add cream and reduce over high heat until slightly thickened. Season with salt and pepper.

Remove sauce from heat and stir in herbs.

Arrange beans on warmed platter and top with salmon, lobster, shrimp, and a spill of sauce.

CHAPTER 7

Poultry and Game Birds

Poultry has always held an honored place on Heartland family tables. Through the early part of this century, chicken or turkey was a luxury reserved for company dinner or other special occasions. Today, thanks to technological advances in production, poultry is abundant and affordable, making it one of the  Midwest's (as well as the nation's), most popular meats. Poultry is versatile, an excellent source of high-quality protein, low in fat and calories.

STEWED CAPON WITH PARSLEY DUMPLINGS

SERVES 6

✳

SUCCULENT, TENDER, MEATY—THAT'S CAPON, A DESEXED MALE CHICKEN THAT IS IDEAL FOR ROASTING, BRAISING, OR STEAMING. BE SURE TO KEEP THE COOKING LIQUID BELOW THE BOIL.

1 capon (about 5 lb)

1/4 cup corn oil

2 cloves garlic, minced

2 onions, sliced

1/2 teaspoon each salt and paprika

4 carrots, peeled and sliced

3 celery stalks, sliced

2 bay leaves

1/2 teaspoon each dried thyme and white pepper

FOR PARSLEY DUMPLINGS:

1/2 cup flour

1/2 cup cream

1/4 cup minced fresh parsley

Remove legs and wings. Split capon in half and cut each half in 4 pieces.

In skillet over medium-high heat, sauté garlic and onions until translucent. Add chicken, sprinkle with salt and paprika and fry, turning until browned, about 5 minutes on each side.

Arrange capon and onions in stockpot. Add carrots, celery, bay leaves, thyme, pepper, and water to cover. Bring to boil over medium heat. Cover partially, reduce heat, and simmer 1 1/2 hours. From time to time skim off fat.

To make dumplings, stir together flour, cream, and parsley. Let stand 5 minutes. Drop by tablespoonfuls onto stew. Cover and cook 5 minutes without lifting lid.

Ladle chicken, vegetables, and broth into heated tureen and float dumplings on top. Discard bay leaves. Serve immediately.

PEKIN FRIED CHICKEN

SERVES 6

✳

PEKIN, IN CENTRAL ILLINOIS, IS IN THE STATE'S PRIME CORN- AND POULTRY-PRODUCING REGION. CRUSTY ON THE OUTSIDE, MOIST AND TENDER ON THE INSIDE, THIS VERSION OF AN ALL-AMERICAN FAVORITE MAKES IT EASY TO PLEASE A CROWD.

3 cups buttermilk

6 boned chicken breast halves, (about 6 oz each), with skin intact

1 can (12 oz) beer

1 1/2 cups flour

1 teaspoon each salt and baking soda

2 eggs, beaten

1/4 teaspoon paprika

Vegetable oil, for frying

Divide buttermilk between 2 large, self-sealing plastic bags. Add 3 chicken breasts to each bag and seal tops securely. Turn bags, coating chicken with buttermilk. Lay bags on tray and refrigerate 3 hours, turning bags over once.

While chicken is marinating, make batter. In deep bowl stir together beer, flour, salt, baking soda, eggs, and paprika. Let stand 30 minutes, then stir again just before using.

Drain chicken. In deep heavy skillet pour in oil to depth of 1 inch. Heat to 375° F. Dip chicken in batter, tapping off excess batter. Slide 3 chicken breasts into oil. Fry until crust is a golden brown, about 2 minutes. Turn chicken over and continue cooking until chicken is brown on all sides and cooked through. To test for doneness remove 1 piece and cut into it. Meat should be whitish throughout. Using slotted spoon remove to paper towels to drain. Place in warm oven. Repeat with remaining chicken.

Serve piping hot.

ROAST CHICKEN, ROOT VEGETABLES, AND CORNBREAD DRESSING

SERVES 6 TO 8

✹

RESTAURANTS IN THE TOWN OF FRANKENMUTH IN SAGINAW COUNTY, MICHIGAN, ARE RENOWNED FOR THEIR CHICKEN DINNERS. BEGUN IN 1848, THE HISTORIC FRANKENMUTH MILL RESUMED GRINDING IN 1982 AFTER A LONG HIATUS. THE MILL GRINDS A DISTINCTIVE LIGHT YELLOW CORN THAT IS IDEAL FOR CORNBREAD.

FOR CORNBREAD DRESSING:

3 cups cornbread, cut in 1/2-inch pieces or crumbled (see page 81)

3 tablespoons bacon drippings

1 clove garlic, minced

1 medium onion, minced

1 cup chopped apple

1 cup chopped celery

1/4 cup minced fresh parsley

1 teaspoon each dried sage and dried marjoram

Preheat oven to 375° F.

To make dressing, place cornbread in mixing bowl. In frying pan over medium heat, warm bacon drippings. Add garlic, onion, apple, and celery and sauté, stirring occasionally, about 5 minutes. Sprinkle with parsley, sage, and marjoram.

Add onion mixture to cornbread and toss well. Place in baking dish and set aside.

Stuff chickens loosely with cornbread dressing and bake remaining stuffing separately. Trim any visible fat from chickens and place, breast side up, in 9-by-13-inch baking dish. Sprinkle chickens with thyme, garlic powder, black pepper, and apple slices. Place chickens and stuffing in oven. Roast chickens and stuffing until thigh joints move easily and juices run clear when birds are pierced with sharp knife, about 1 hour. Baste the stuffing mixture with drippings from time to time.

While chickens are cooking, bring saucepan three-fourths full of salted water to boil. Add turnips and parsnips, reduce heat to medium, and cook 5 minutes. Drain.

In large frying pan over medium heat, melt butter. Add drained vegetables and sauté over medium heat, stirring occasionally, until lightly browned and fork tender. Sprinkle with salt, fennel seed, and white pepper.

2 fryer or broiler chickens (2 1/2 lbs each), any visible fat discarded, washed, patted dry
1/2 teaspoon each ground thyme and garlic powder
1/4 teaspoon black pepper
2 apples, peeled, cored, and sliced

3 turnips, peeled and cut into wedges
3 parsnips, peeled and cut into quarters
1/4 cup (1/2 stick) butter or margarine
1/2 teaspoon salt
1/2 teaspoon fennel seed
2 teaspoons white pepper
2 tablespoons minced fresh parsley

Remove chickens to warmed serving platter. Arrange sautéed vegetables around chickens. Sprinkle with parsley. Serve hot with dressing.

TERRINE OF CHICKEN AND WILD MUSHROOMS

SERVES 8 TO 10

✹

CHEF-OWNER THIERRY LEFEUVRE OF FROGGY'S FRENCH CAFE, HIGHWOOD, ILLINOIS, CREATED THIS DELICIOUS DISH USING PRODUCTS SELECTED FROM THE HEARTLAND. ON HIS MENU ONE FINDS FRESH PUMPKIN TART, TERRINE OF WILD MUSHROOMS, AND DISHES GARNISHED WITH NASTURTIUM FLOWERS. THIS CREATIVE BRETON CHEF'S ORIGINAL RECIPE CALLS FOR SHIITAKE MUSHROOMS, BUT MICHIGAN MORELS OR CHANTERELLES COULD ALSO BE USED.

6 tablespoons extra virgin olive oil

2 ounces shallots, minced

1 pound fresh shiitake mushrooms, stemmed

1 teaspoon salt

1/2 teaspoon minced fresh basil

1/2 teaspoon pepper, divided

4 cups chopped, cooked chicken

8 ounces spinach, trimmed, washed, well drained

2 cups whipping cream, chilled

16 thin slices (12 oz) bacon (not hickory flavored), blanched

Preheat oven to 325° F.

In large heavy skillet over medium heat, warm olive oil. Add shallots and mushrooms and sauté 5 minutes. Sprinkle with 1/2 teaspoon of the salt, basil, and a little pepper. Remove from heat and set aside.

In food processor fitted with steel blade, combine half of the chicken, half of the spinach, and half of the remaining salt and pepper. Purée using 4 short pulses, each followed by 10-second pause. With machine running, pour half of the cream through feed tube and process until combined. Repeat with remaining chicken, spinach, salt, pepper, and cream. In bowl combine batches.

Arrange bacon in slightly overlapping rows across a 5-by-9-by-3-inch nonstick bread pan, allowing ends of bacon slices to overhang edges of pan.

Spoon 1/4-inch-thick layer of the chicken mixture over bacon to anchor mushrooms. Arrange one third of the mushrooms in a layer over the chicken. Alternate layers of chicken and mushrooms, finishing with a layer of chicken mixture smoothed over the top. Bring strips of bacon over terrine.

Place pan in larger baking pan. Pour hot water into larger pan to depth of 2 inches. Cover with sheet of buttered aluminum foil, buttered side in. Cook until tester inserted in center comes out clean, about 1 hour.

Remove to rack and cool completely. Refrigerate overnight or at least 8 hours.

To serve, invert onto serving platter, lift off pan, and slice thinly.

FARMHOUSE CHICKEN POT PIE WITH DILL PASTRY

SERVES 6

❉

CHICKEN IS ESPECIALLY POPULAR IN THE MIDWEST, WITH ILLINOIS AND INDIANA AMONG THE NATION'S TOP PRODUCERS. ITS MILD FLAVOR LENDS ITSELF TO THE ADDITION OF HERBS AND SPICES; FOR EXAMPLE, FRAGRANT DILL PERMEATES THE PASTRY OF THIS OLD-TIME FAVORITE CHICKEN RECIPE. USE HOMEMADE CHICKEN STOCK FOR THE BEST RESULTS. IF YOU LIKE, PREPARE INDIVIDUAL SERVINGS IN RAMEKINS. COLE SLAW IS A GOOD ACCOMPANIMENT.

FOR DILL PASTRY:

2 1/4 cups flour

1/4 cup chopped fresh dill

1/2 teaspoon salt

1/3 cup vegetable shortening, cut into 1/2-inch pieces

1 tablespoon white vinegar

4 to 6 tablespoons ice water

To make pastry, combine flour, dill, salt, and shortening in food processor fitted with steel blade. Process 10 seconds. With machine running add vinegar and water through the tube and process until dough ball forms around center post, 45 to 60 seconds. Gather dough into ball and wrap in plastic wrap. Refrigerate 1 hour.

Preheat oven to 375° F.

To make filling, bring saucepan three-fourths full of salted water to boil. Add celery, onion, and carrot and cook on medium heat until just tender, about 15 minutes. Drain well and set aside.

In separate saucepan over medium heat, melt butter. Whisk in flour and cook, stirring until flour is absorbed, about 3 minutes. Slowly whisk in chicken stock, half-and-half, salt, rosemary, pepper, and parsley. Continue to cook and stir until mixture thickens, about 4 minutes. Stir in cooked vegetables, chicken, mushrooms, and peas.

To make pie, divide dough in half. On lightly floured board roll out each half into round 10 inches in diameter. Place 1 dough round in bottom of 9-inch pie plate. Bake crust 5 minutes. Cool. Prick bottom with fork.

Spoon chicken filling into prebaked crust. Add top crust, seal edges, and cut 1/2-inch vent in center of crust.

Bake 35 to 40 minutes or until crust is firm and lightly browned. Cool 5 minutes before serving.

FOR FILLING:

1 cup thinly sliced celery

1 large onion, chopped

1 large carrot, grated

6 tablespoons (3/4 stick) butter or margarine

3 tablespoons flour

1/2 cup chicken stock

1 cup half-and-half

1/2 teaspoon each salt and dried rosemary

1/4 teaspoon white pepper

4 tablespoons chopped fresh parsley

2 1/2 cups diced, cooked chicken

1/2 pound fresh button mushrooms, trimmed

1 package (10 oz) frozen peas, thawed and drained

Free-Range Chicken with Blueberry Muffin Stuffing

SERVES 4

✳

KAY ZUBOW, A COFOUNDER OF THE HEARTLAND FOOD SOCIETY AND OWNER OF WILD GAME, INC., HAS BEEN A PIONEER IN PROMOTING AND DISTRIBUTING GAME AND GAME PRODUCTS TO RESTAURANTS AND THE PUBLIC. FREE-RANGE CHICKENS, POUSSINS, AND MALLARDS ARE AMONG WILD GAME'S OFFERINGS. SEE PAGE 237.

THE BLUEBERRY MUFFIN RECIPE ON PAGE 88 PROVIDES THE PRIME INGREDIENT FOR THE STUFFING IN THIS DISH.

FOR MUFFIN STUFFING:

6 blueberry muffins (see page 88)

1/4 cup (1/2 stick) butter or margarine

1 onion, coarsely chopped

1 cup sliced fresh mushrooms

1 free-range chicken (3 1/2 to 4 lb)

2 tablespoons butter or margarine

1/4 teaspoon salt

1/4 teaspoon white pepper

1 teaspoon dried marjoram

1 cup fresh blueberries

To make stuffing, crumble muffins into deep bowl. In a skillet over medium heat, melt butter. Add onion and mushrooms and sauté, stirring often, until tender, about 5 minutes. Cool. Stir cooled vegetables into crumbled muffins. You should have about 3 cups stuffing.

Preheat oven to 350° F.

Trim any visible fat from chicken and place, breast side up, on counter with cavity facing you. Working from cavity opening, loosen skin around breast area of chicken. You will be able to extend loose skin to leg without tearing it.

Carefully spoon stuffing under skin, then gently pat skin back into shape. Brush chicken with remaining butter. Sprinkle with salt, pepper, and marjoram.

Place chicken on rack, breast side up, in roasting pan. Pour water to depth of 1/4 to 1/2 inch in pan. Roast chicken until thigh joints move easily and juices run clear when bird is pierced with sharp knife, 65 to 75 minutes.

Let chicken stand 10 minutes before carving. Place on serving platter. Sprinkle with blueberries. Carve in kitchen or at table.

BUTTERFLIED POUSSIN WITH GARLIC CHIPS

❋

ORIGINALLY FROM FRANCE, POUSSIN IS A SPECIALTY BREED OF YOUNG CHICKEN UNDER 6 WEEKS OLD AND WEIGHING ONLY 10 TO 18 OUNCES.

FOR CORN RELISH:

3 cups fresh corn kernels

1 each red bell pepper, seeded and chopped, and onion, minced

3/4 cup chopped celery

3 tablespoons sugar

1/2 cup cider vinegar

1/2 teaspoon each salt, celery seed, and dry mustard

6 poussins (about 10 oz each), butterflied

6 tablespoons (3/4 stick) butter or margarine, at room temperature

1/2 teaspoon salt

1 teaspoon dried tarragon

1/4 teaspoon pepper

2 cups canola oil

4 elephant garlic cloves, sliced paper-thin lengthwise

To make relish, combine relish ingredients in saucepan. Place over medium heat and bring to simmer. Cover and simmer, stirring occasionally, 10 to 12 minutes. Cool and ladle into bowl. Cover and refrigerate until serving.

Preheat oven to 375° F.

Rub poussins with butter. Sprinkle with salt, tarragon, and pepper. Arrange on aluminum foil-lined baking sheet. Bake until juices run clear when pierced with a sharp knife, 20 to 30 minutes. Let stand 5 minutes, then remove to warmed platter.

While poussins are cooking, in deep saucepan, heat oil to 375° F. Working in 1/2-cup batches, fry garlic about 1 1/2 minutes and drain on paper towels. Keep in warm oven until all chips are cooked.

Sprinkle garlic chips over and around poussins. Serve immediately with corn relish.

SMOKED TURKEY BREAST WITH GINGER-PEANUT SAUCE

SERVES 6 TO 8

❋

ALTHOUGH THE MIDWEST IS HOME TO A TRADITIONAL CUISINE WITH FRENCH, GERMAN, SCANDINAVIAN, ITALIAN, POLISH, AND MEXICAN INFLUENCES, A SECOND WAVE OF IMMIGRATION HAS INTRODUCED CHINESE, THAI, VIETNAMESE, KOREAN, AND OTHER SOUTHEAST ASIAN FOODS AND FLAVORS. IN THIS RECIPE TURKEY FROM THE HEARTLAND TEAMS UP WITH AN ASIAN-STYLE SAUCE.

1 turkey breast (about 3 1/2 lb), boned with skin intact

Light olive oil

Garlic powder

3 mesquite chunks, soaked in water 30 minutes and drained

FOR GINGER-PEANUT SAUCE:

1 cup smooth peanut butter

1 cup mayonnaise

1/3 cup beer

2 tablespoons soy sauce

1 tablespoon ground ginger

1/4 teaspoon hot-pepper flakes

3 green onions, minced

Rub turkey breast with olive oil and sprinkle with garlic powder. Set aside.

Prepare smoker according to manufacturer's instructions. Fill charcoal pan three-fourths full with briquets and light. When coals are partly ashen, after about 20 minutes, add mesquite to charcoal. Fill water pan with boiling water.

Set turkey breast on top rack of smoker. Cover and smoke 1 1/2 to 2 hours, checking coals every 40 minutes to see if they need to be replenished. Turkey breast is done when juices run clear when meat is pierced.

Remove turkey to cutting board and let stand for 10 minutes. Discard skin and slice turkey.

To prepare sauce, in food processor fitted with steel blade, combine all ingredients. Process until smooth. Spoon into bowl. Serve sliced turkey with sauce on side.

TURKEY—AMERICA'S CULINARY GIFT TO THE WORLD

Turkeys are native to the Americas. Large tough birds, wild turkeys once roamed North and South America, pecking for food and roosting in trees. Larger than the peacock, they also were fast. If the situation demanded it, a turkey could both fly and run at great speed.

By the time Hernando Cortez brought domesticated turkeys back to Spain from Mexico in 1519, the Mayas and Incas had been raising them for close to five hundred years. According to Midwest food authority Waverley Root, this may not have been by choice. Turkeys apparently were so clever at raiding grain supplies, it is said, that having been unsuccessful at securing their grain stores, the Native Americans resorted to penning the birds, which necessitated their providing the turkeys with food and water.

The great patriot Ben Franklin proposed the turkey as our national symbol. Today, the turkey is recognized everywhere as one of America's great gifts to the culinary world. In Indiana, where the Perdue turkey operation is headquartered, Turkey Run State Park is named for the area's great flocks of wild turkeys.

SMOKED TURKEY WITH STEWED FRUITS

SERVES 12

✳

PREPARED IN THIS MANNER, TURKEY IS TENDER AND FLAVORFUL. SERVE COLD FOR A LARGE GATHERING.

3 apple or cherry tree twigs or hickory chips

1 turkey (12 lb)

FOR STEWED FRUITS:

2 cups pitted prunes

1 cup dried apricots

1 cup mixed dried fruit such as apples, pears, and the like

1 cup applejack brandy

3/4 cup sugar

1 lemon, thinly sliced

3 gingersnap cookies, crumbled

Soak twigs or chips 30 minutes in water to cover; drain. Meanwhile, prepare smoker according to manufacturer's guidelines. Fill charcoal pan two-thirds full and heat until ashen. Scatter drained twigs or hickory chips over hot coals. Fill water pan two-thirds full with hot water.

Trim any visible fat from turkey; remove giblets and neck for another use. Set turkey on top rack of smoker. Cover and smoke 6 to 8 hours. Turkey is done when thigh joints move easily and juices run clear when meat is pierced.

While turkey is smoking, prepare stewed fruits. Arrange all dried fruits in saucepan. Pour in brandy. Add water to cover and let stand 30 minutes. Mix in sugar and lemon slices. Place over medium heat and bring to simmer. Simmer, stirring occasionally until fruits are tender, about 30 minutes, adding cookies after first 10 minutes. Ladle fruits into container and cool. Cover and refrigerate until serving.

Let turkey stand at room temperature 10 to 15 minutes before carving. Serve warm or cold with fruits.

TURKEY WITH PEACH STUFFING

SERVES 12 TO 14

❋

PLACING STUFFING UNDER THE SKIN HELPS FLAVOR THE TURKEY AND KEEPS IT MOIST. PASS PEACH BUTTER (SEE PAGE 173) AT THE TABLE FOR GUESTS TO ENJOY WITH THE TURKEY AND STUFFING.

To make stuffing, in saucepan combine giblets and neck with water to cover. Bring to boil, reduce heat to low, and simmer until tender, about 20 minutes. Drain and cool, remove meat from neck bones, and mince along with giblets.

Meanwhile, in large skillet over medium heat, melt butter. Add onion and carrot and sauté, stirring occasion-

FOR PEACH STUFFING:

Giblets and neck from turkey

1/4 cup (1/2 stick) butter or margarine

1 onion, minced

1 carrot, peeled and grated

1/2 cup dried cranberries

1 can (16 oz) peaches, drained and chopped, or 2 cups peeled, chopped fresh or thawed frozen peaches

4 to 5 cups roughly cut whole-grain bread cubes

1/2 teaspoon each salt, ground cinnamon, dried thyme, and dried sage

1/4 teaspoon pepper

1 turkey (12 to 14 lb)

1 large onion, thinly sliced

1 large carrot, peeled and sliced

3 tablespoons vegetable shortening or margarine, at room temperature

3/4 teaspoon each paprika and garlic powder

Peach Butter (see page 173)

ally, 5 minutes. Add minced meat and continue cooking, stirring occasionally, 5 minutes longer. Stir in cranberries and peaches. In large bowl place bread cubes. Add giblet mixture, salt, cinnamon, thyme, sage, and pepper. Toss well.

Preheat oven to 325° F. Trim any visible fat from turkey and discard.

Pour water into roasting pan to depth of 1/4 inch. Add onion and carrot. Place rack in pan and set turkey, breast side up, on rack. Working from cavity opening, loosen skin around breast area. Carefully spoon stuffing under skin, then gently pat skin back into shape. Brush turkey with shortening. Sprinkle with paprika and garlic powder. Cover loosely with aluminum foil, securing ends of foil before cooking.

Roast turkey 3 hours; remove foil and baste turkey with pan drippings. Continue roasting until turkey is golden brown in color and juices run clear when pierced with a sharp knife, about 1 hour longer, or until turkey registers 185° to 190° F when thermometer is inserted into thickest area of thigh, being careful not to touch bone.

Let turkey stand at room temperature 10 to 15 minutes before carving.

GAME BIRDS, FARM-RAISED AND WILD

Learning the lore of the edible wild was a skill the first settlers of the Heartland—and before them the trailblazers and trappers—could ill afford to overlook. Although nowadays seeking out such provender is more of a hobby than a necessity, the Midwest still boasts of wild game in its forests and fields.

Rich in flavor, high in protein and nutritious minerals, and low in fat, game birds are a delightful change of pace for the diner as well as the cook. Some game birds can be purchased from commercial outlets (see pages 236 and 237), while the more unusual varieties are available only through a hunter's generosity.

Indiana is a significant supplier of duck, and Illinois boasts the largest mallard duck hatchery in the nation. Wild quail, pheasant, partridge, and turkey glean the fields following the grain harvests in the Midwest, particularly the miles of rich grain fields in Iowa.

The woods and fields of Michigan are thick with game, bringing hunters from afar to test their skills. Wild fowl, such as ducks and geese, ring-necked pheasants, and partridge fill the tables of wild game banquets in Wisconsin.

The province of Ontario along the Canadian Corridor also is a hunter's paradise, providing many varieties of wild fowl for sport and fine dining.

Wisconsin ruffed grouse, Illinois quail, Indiana ducklings and turkeys, and Michigan pheasant are delicious, lean alternatives to more traditional meats. Succulent game, both wild and farm-raised, is in growing demand as an export, even as milder, more abundant poultry such as chicken and turkey makes its way with greater frequency to Heartland tables.

HONEY-ROASTED DUCK WITH SAUERKRAUT

SERVES 4

✳

WISCONSIN IS CREDITED AS THE TOP U.S. PRODUCER OF SAUERKRAUT, A TRADITIONAL HEARTLAND FOIL FOR THE RICHNESS OF DUCK. TOASTING THE JUNIPER BERRIES BRIEFLY IN A WARM SKILLET BRINGS OUT THEIR FRAGRANCE.

SERVE THIS DISH WITH POTA-TO PANCAKES (SEE PAGE 162).

1 duck (about 5 lb)

3 cups drained sauerkraut

1 teaspoon juniper berries (optional)

2 tablespoons caraway seed

3 tablespoons clover or wildflower honey (preferably from the Heartland)

Preheat oven to 425° F. Trim any visible fat from duck. Reserve duck giblets for another use.

Place sauerkraut in bowl. Add juniper berries (if using) and caraway seed and toss to mix well. Spoon sauerkraut mixture into duck cavity and close with skewers. Prick duck all over with fork tines. Spread honey over duck.

In roasting pan pour in water to depth of 1/4 to 1/2 inch of water. Place rack in pan and place duck, breast side up, on rack. Roast duck uncovered 1 hour. Reduce heat to 325° F. Continue roasting for 1 hour and 40 minutes, pricking duck again during roast-ing. Duck is well done when skin turns golden brown and thigh joints move easily.

Remove to warmed serving platter and let stand 10 minutes before carving. Serve hot.

MALLARD WITH CRANBERRIES

SERVES 4

❋

WHISTLING WINGS IS A 350-ACRE FARM IN NORTHWESTERN ILLINOIS THAT BREEDS AND RAISES MALLARD DUCKS IN SUCH QUANTITY THAT IT HAS PUT THE TINY TOWN OF HANOVER (POPULATION 1,100) ON THE MAP AS THE MALLARD CAPITAL OF THE WORLD. MORE THAN THIRTY-NINE YEARS AGO, WHEN LEO WHALEN PURCHASED THE PROPERTY, IT WAS A CORNFIELD. TODAY, THOUSANDS OF YOUNG DUCKS SWIM THERE ON SPRING-FED PONDS.

In bowl combine all marinade ingredients. Divide between 2 large, self-sealing plastic bags. Trim any visible fat from ducks. Place 1 mallard in each bag and seal tops securely. Place bags on tray and marinate mallards 2 hours at room temperature, turning bags twice.

Remove ducks from marinade and drain. Cut into quarters. Sprinkle pieces with flour.

In large heavy skillet over medium-high heat, melt butter. Add mallards and sauté

FOR MARINADE:

1/2 cup olive oil

3/4 cup red wine

2 bay leaves

1/4 teaspoon pepper

1/2 teaspoon dried thyme

2 mallards (2 lb each)

1/4 cup flour

3 tablespoons butter or margarine

1/3 cup water

2 cups canned cranberry relish

1/4 teaspoon ground cloves

1 stick cinnamon

Cranberry juice or additional water, if needed

1/3 cup dried cranberries

until browned, about 2 minutes on each side. Meanwhile, in bowl stir together water, cranberry relish, cloves, and cinnamon stick. Add to pan, reduce heat to medium-low, cover partially, and simmer until mallards are fork tender, about 30 minutes. Add cranberry juice or water if pan begins to dry.

Remove mallard pieces to warmed serving dish. Sprinkle with dried cranberries. Drizzle drippings over mallards. Serve hot.

SAUTÉED DUCK BREASTS WITH RED CABBAGE AND RASPBERRY SAUCE

SERVES 4

❉

IF YOU HAVE EATEN DUCK LATELY, CHANCES ARE IT WAS HATCHED, RAISED, PROCESSED, AND SHIPPED AT MAPLE LEAF FARMS IN INDIANA. FOUNDED IN 1958, THE COMPANY BEGAN BY SHIPPING ABOUT 5,400 BIRDS A WEEK. IN 1991, THE COMPANY SHIPPED 12 MILLION DUCKS TO CUSTOMERS ALL OVER THE WORLD. MAPLE LEAF FARMS DUCKS ARE RAISED UNCAGED IN LARGE BUILDINGS IN WHICH TEMPERATURE, LIGHT, AND HUMIDITY ARE REGULATED FOR MAXIMUM COMFORT. THE BIRDS' FEED ALSO IS GROWN ON COMPANY FARMS. AS A RESULT OF THIS OPTIMUM ENVIRONMENT, DUCKS REACH THEIR FULL GROWTH OF ABOUT 6 1/2 POUNDS IN A SHORT TIME.

FOR RASPBERRY SAUCE:

1 packet duck or chicken giblets

3 tablespoons butter or margarine

3 shallots, minced

1 tablespoon flour

3/4 cup dry white wine

3 tablespoons cherry jelly

2 cups frozen raspberries, defrosted, with juice

1/2 teaspoon dried mint

To make sauce, in saucepan combine giblets with water to cover. Bring to boil, reduce heat to medium-low, and simmer until tender, about 20 minutes. Drain, reserving 1/2 cup liquid. When cool, remove meat from bones and mince meat along with giblets. Set aside.

In saucepan over medium heat, melt butter. Add shallots and sauté 3 minutes. Whisk in flour and wine and bring to boil. Reduce heat to simmer and cook about 5 minutes. Strain and return liquid to pan. Add reserved 1/2 cup liquid from giblets. Cook 3 minutes over medium heat. Stir in jelly and whisk until melted. Add raspberries and juice and mint. Simmer, stirring, about 4 minutes.

To make duck breasts, in bowl stir together flour, salt, and pepper. Dredge duck with seasoned flour.

In large heavy skillet over medium heat, warm oil. Add duck and sauté 2 minutes on each side. Add wine to pan, cover, and cook until done to taste, 10 to 12 minutes. Duck is well done when juices run clear when pierced with sharp knife.

FOR DUCK BREASTS:

1/2 cup flour

1/4 teaspoon each salt and white pepper

2 duck breasts (7 to 8 oz each)

3 tablespoons canola or vegetable oil

1/2 cup red wine or other full-bodied wine

FOR RED CABBAGE:

3 tablespoons canola oil

1 head red cabbage, cored, thinly sliced (about 6 cups)

1/4 cup red wine

1/3 cup red wine vinegar

1/3 cup sugar

1/3 cup raisins

To prepare cabbage, in saucepan over medium heat, warm oil. Add cabbage and sauté, stirring often, until wilted, about 5 minutes. Add wine and continue cooking over medium heat until tender, about 5 minutes. Add vinegar, sugar, and raisins and stir to combine. Cover and continue cooking 10 minutes.

To serve, spoon small amount of raspberry sauce on each plate. Set duck over sauce. Place spoonful of cabbage alongside.

BRAISED PHEASANT WITH CHERRY CIDER SAUCE

SERVES 4

✹

A TRIO OF CHERRY FLAVORS—SWEET CHERRY WINE, CHERRY JELLY, AND DRIED CHERRIES—COMPLEMENT THE SUCCULENCE OF BRAISED PHEASANT.

3 tablespoons butter or margarine

3 tablespoons canola oil

1 large onion, thinly sliced

2 pheasants (about 2 1/2 lbs each), split in half

2 cloves garlic, minced

1/2 teaspoon dried rosemary

1/4 cup minced fresh parsley

2 tablespoons cherry wine or other sweet wine

FOR CHERRY CIDER SAUCE:

1/4 cup (1/2 stick) butter or margarine

2 tablespoons cornstarch

3/4 cup pheasant or chicken stock or water

1 cup apple cider

1/2 cup cherry or crabapple jelly, or 1/4 cup each

1/2 cup dried cherries

In large heavy skillet over medium heat, melt butter and oil. Add onion and sauté until translucent, about 5 minutes. Add pheasant halves and sauté until browned, 2 minutes on each side. Sprinkle with garlic, rosemary, and parsley. Stir in wine. Cover and simmer over low heat basting every 5 minutes with pan juices until tender, about 30 minutes.

While pheasant is cooking, make sauce. In saucepan over medium heat, melt butter. Whisk in cornstarch. Slowly stir in stock, cider, and jelly and continue cooking and stirring until mixture thickens slightly, about 4 minutes. Add cherries and cook 5 minutes longer.

Arrange pheasant halves on warmed serving platter and drizzle with sauce. Bring to table piping hot.

CHAPTER 8

Stockyard Specialties and Game Meats

"Where's the beef?" Most Americans know the answer: in the Heartland, of course. Pork is another food product synonymous with the Heartland. Midwesterners like "the other white meat" prepared in a variety of ways, from spicy hot ribs to sophis-  ticated pork medallions served with mush- rooms. Veal and lamb also are popular in the Midwest, and both farm-raised buffalo (bison) and venison are available commercially in many areas of the Heartland.

STEAK ON A BED OF GREENS

SERVES 4

❋

EVEN IN THE HEARTLAND, BEEF NEEDN'T ALWAYS BE A HEAVY MAIN-DISH COURSE. THIS DISH MAKES A DELIGHTFUL ENTRÉE FOR A LIGHT SUPPER.

4 steaks (5 to 6 ounces each)
Salt and freshly ground pepper, to taste
3/4 cup extra virgin olive oil, divided
1 cup thinly sliced red onion
1/2 cup sliced yellow or red bell pepper
1 cup sliced mushrooms
1 cup broccoli florets, blanched and drained
1 cup sliced carrots, blanched and drained
3 cloves garlic, minced
1 cup beef stock
1 tablespoon minced mixed fresh herbs such as thyme,
*   marjoram, basil, and sage*
6 to 8 cups mixed salad greens
2 tablespoons balsamic vinegar

Season steaks with salt and pepper. In a skillet over high heat, warm 2 tablespoons of the oil. Add steaks and sauté, turning once, until cooked to desired doneness. Remove and keep warm.

Wipe out pan, add 1/4 cup of the oil and warm over medium heat. Add onion, bell pepper, and mushrooms and sauté until tender. Add broccoli and carrots and toss over high heat until heated through.

Remove vegetables from pan and set aside. Add garlic, stock, and herbs to pan and simmer 3 minutes to blend flavors. Divide sauce evenly among individual plates.

Place salad greens in large bowl. Add sautéed vegetables, remaining olive oil, and vinegar. Toss well and divide among plates. Slice warm steak and arrange on top of salad. Pass the pepper mill.

STEAK CHICAGO-STYLE

At one time Chicago was the largest marketplace for livestock in the United States. The city's stockyards took in live cattle and other beasts on the hoof from all over the country. Fresh meats—fillets, steaks, chops, roasts—were shipped all over the country. An estimated 600 million beef cattle were processed between 1865 and 1971 (the last year of the stockyards' full operation).

Not suprisingly, for years, the basic dining establishment in the Chicago area was the steakhouse. A few old-style steakhouses still operate, such as Gene and Georgetti's, That Steak Joynt, Eli's, Morton's, and others. In the past, the typical Chicago steakhouse diner might devour a pound or two of steak at one sitting and afterward polish off several whiskeys and a cigar. The average porterhouse cut weighed more than twenty-two ounces, measured six by eight inches, and was at least an inch and a half thick. Each order was garnished with parsley and accompanied by a few steak fries or a baked potato, along with sautéed or broiled mushrooms. Not a speck of blank plate could be seen beneath the mountains of food.

Over the last ten years, eating habits have changed enough to force many steakhouses out of business. Midwesterners have heard enough about cholesterol and fat intake to reconsider their devotion to huge portions of well-marbled meat. But few people raised on prime aged steak every Saturday night are willing to give up the pleasure entirely. Today, however, a six-ounce portion is considered sufficient for the average diner.

MY FAVORITE STEAK

SERVES 6

✳

EVEN AFTER YEARS OF COOKING STEAKS FOR MILLIONS OF CUSTOMERS, BILLY SIEGEL, PROPRI-
ETOR OF THAT STEAK JOYNT IN CHICAGO, STILL LIKES TO PREPARE STEAK AT HOME. ALTHOUGH
HE WOULD NOT DIVULGE THE INGREDIENTS OF HIS SECRET MARINADE, SIEGEL AGREED TO
SHARE HIS METHOD AND MENU.

Take a strip steak and trim well, until no fat is visible. *6 Chicago strip steaks (15 to 16 oz each)*
Grill outside over ashen coals to the desired degree ("I like my steaks rare, " Siegel says).

He continues: "Serve with sweet potatoes, steamed peapods, okra with lemon, and a salad of hearts of palms and artichoke hearts tossed in a basic olive oil vinaigrette, with as much Champagne as your guests can drink."

VEGETABLE-STUFFED BREAST OF VEAL

SERVES 6

❋

ALTHOUGH THIS DISH IS ROAST-
ED UNCOVERED, THE ADDITION
OF LIQUID TO THE ROASTING
PAN HELPS KEEP THE VEAL
MOIST AS IT COOKS.

2 tablespoons butter or margarine

2 tablespoons extra virgin olive oil

2 large onions, minced

1 large carrot, peeled and grated

1 cup chopped celery

1/2 teaspoon salt

1/2 teaspoon minced garlic

1/4 teaspoon pepper

6 slices day-old oatmeal bread, crusts discarded, cut into
  1/2-inch cubes

Breast of veal (4 to 6 lb), deep pocket cut in side, and fat
  trimmed

Preheat oven to 325° F.

In heavy skillet over medium heat, melt butter with oil. Add half of onion, the carrot, and celery and sauté, stirring often, 5 minutes. Season with salt, garlic, and pepper and add bread cubes. Cook over medium heat, tossing, 3 minutes.

Spoon vegetable mixture into veal pocket. Pour 1/2 to 1/4 inch water in bottom of roasting pan and set rack in pan. Place veal on rack. Scatter remaining onion into water.

Roast uncovered until tender, 20 minutes per pound. Cool 10 minutes, then slice, using ribs as guide. Arrange on platter and serve hot.

SAUERBRATEN

SERVES 8

❋

SOME RECIPES FOR THIS DISH OF GERMAN ORIGIN CALL FOR THE ADDITION OF BAY LEAVES AND CARAWAY SEEDS TO THE MARINADE, AND FOR LEAVING THE MEAT IN THE VINEGAR SOLUTION FOR AS LONG AS FOUR DAYS. TRADITIONALISTS OFTEN INCORPORATE RAISINS AND CRUSHED GINGER-SNAPS INTO THE SAUCE MADE FROM THE MARINADE. BUTTERED NOODLES, SPAETZLE (SEE PAGE 166), OR POTATO DUMPLINGS ARE TRADITIONAL ACCOMPANIMENTS.

1 beef rump or bottom roast (about 3 lbs)

2 large cloves garlic, cut in half

1/2 teaspoon salt

1/4 teaspoon freshly ground pepper

6 whole cloves

1 large onion, thinly sliced

1/2 cup chopped celery

FOR MARINADE:

2 cups red wine vinegar

2 1/4 cups water

1/4 cup sugar

3 tablespoons butter or margarine

FOR SAUCE:

3 tablespoons firmly packed light brown sugar

1 3/4 cups marinade, reserved

1/2 cup water

1 cup sour cream or plain yogurt

Rub meat with cut surface of garlic. Sprinkle with salt and pepper. Place in large ceramic or glass dish. Sprinkle with cloves, onion, and celery.

To make marinade, combine vinegar, water, and sugar in saucepan. Bring to boil over medium heat. Immediately pour marinade over meat. Cool. Cover bowl and refrigerate for up to 48 hours, turning meat once or twice a day.

Drain meat and pat dry. Reserve and strain marinade. In heavy 3-quart pan over medium-high heat, melt butter. Add meat and brown well on all sides. Pour strained marinade over meat, cover, reduce heat to simmer, and cook until meat is fork tender, about 2 3/4 hours.

Remove meat to platter. Set aside 1 3/4 cups marinade to use for sauce. Let meat stand 10 minutes.

Meanwhile, make sauce. In saucepan over low heat, melt brown sugar until it begins to caramelize. Slowly stir in marinade and water, then remove from heat. Stir in sour cream. You should have about 2 1/4 cups. Taste and adjust seasoning.

Thinly slice meat and arrange on platter. Drizzle some sauce over top. Pass remaining sauce at table.

MEDALLIONS OF PORK WITH MUSHROOMS

SERVES 4

❋

LOCATED IN NEWTON, IOWA, KAY OWEN'S RESTAURANT AND LACORSETT'S MAISON INN ARE HOUSED IN A TURN-OF-THE-CENTURY MISSION-STYLE MANSION. SHE OFFERS SUMPTUOUS SERV-INGS OF HAUTE CUISINE SUCH AS THIS DISH WITH GENEROUS PORTIONS OF HEARTLAND HOSPITALITY.

8 tablespoons (1 stick) butter

1 to 1 1/4 pounds pork tenderloin, cut into 1-inch-thick slices

1/4 cup Cognac

1/4 cup dry white wine

1/2 cup beef stock

2 cups whipping cream

Salt and freshly ground pepper, to taste

1 pound fresh mushrooms, sliced

Chopped fresh parsley, for garnish

In heavy skillet over medium-high heat, melt 5 tablespoons of the butter. Add medallions and cook until barely done, turning once. Transfer to dish and keep warm.

Add Cognac and wine to pan and stir to dislodge any browned bits. Add cream, bring to simmer, and reduce until thickened to sauce consistency. Add salt and pepper.

While sauce thickens, melt remaining 3 tablespoons butter in skillet over medium-high heat. Add mushrooms and sauté until tender, about 5 minutes. Divide medallions among individual plates. Spoon on sauce and top with mushrooms. Garnish with parsley.

GRILLED IOWA PORK CHOPS WITH ROASTED ELEPHANT GARLIC

SERVES 6

❋

ELEPHANT GARLIC (ALLIUM AMPELOPRASUM) IS A DIFFERENT SPECIES OF ALLIUM FROM TRUE GARLIC (ALLIUM SATIVUM) AND HAS MUCH LARGER CLOVES AND A MILDER FLAVOR. THE BUTTERY ROASTED GARLIC PERFECTLY COMPLEMENTS GRAIN-FED IOWA PORK.

6 double-cut pork chops (8 to 10 oz each and 2 in. thick)
Canola or vegetable oil, to brush on chops and garlic
1/2 teaspoon celery seed
6 large bay leaves
2 cups corn cob stems or apple wood chips, soaked 30 minutes in water to cover and drained (optional)
12 cloves elephant garlic

Brush chops with oil and sprinkle with celery seed. Lay 1 bay leaf on top of each chop. Set aside.

Prepare fire in charcoal grill. Coals should be ashen and in two piles. Sprinkle cob stems (if using) over hot coals. Arrange chops in center of greased grill rack so they cook by indirect heat. Cook chops for about 15 minutes, turning every 5 minutes. To test for doneness, remove one chop and cut meat slightly to see if pink color has gone.

While chops are grilling, brush garlic cloves with oil and place at outer edge of grill. Grill about 20 minutes, rotating cloves every 5 to 6 minutes. To serve, place 2 cloves on each dish next to chop. Show guests how to squeeze out garlic and spread over chops.

Note: To prepare indoors, preheat oven to 325° F. Sprinkle chops with salt and pepper and dust lightly with flour. Heat 3 tablespoons butter in nonstick skillet. Add chops and cook 1 1/2 to 2 minutes on each side. Transfer to baking pan and place in oven 15 to 20 minutes, or until knife inserted into thick area of chop shows pink is gone. Roast garlic along with chops.

Oven-Barbecued Ribs

SERVES 6 TO 8

❋

BABY BACK RIBS BENEFIT FROM A SPICY TOMATO BARBECUE SAUCE WARMED UP WITH CHILI POW-
DER AND RED AND BLACK PEPPER. BE SURE TO PROVIDE PLENTY OF NAPKINS AND EXPECT YOUR
GUESTS TO LICK THEIR FINGERS.

FOR SAUCE:

3 slices bacon, cut into small pieces

1 cup minced green onion

3 cloves garlic, minced

3/4 cup catsup

1 can (16 oz) chopped tomatoes

1/4 cup red wine vinegar

1/3 cup firmly packed dark brown sugar

2 teaspoons chili powder

1/8 teaspoon ground cloves

1 teaspoon grated orange zest

Juice from 1 orange

1/2 teaspoon salt

1/4 teaspoon each hot pepper flakes and black pepper

6 pounds baby back ribs, in slabs

1/2 teaspoon liquid mesquite smoke (optional)

To make sauce, in heavy saucepan fry bacon. Leave bacon in pan and discard all but 3 tablespoons of drippings. Add onion and garlic and sauté 3 minutes. Add all remaining sauce ingredients and simmer over medium heat, stirring occasionally, 10 minutes. Taste and adjust seasoning. Remove from heat.

Preheat oven to 325° F.

Bring water in steamer pan to boil. Place rib slabs on rack, cover steamer, and steam for 10 minutes. Remove ribs. Set roasting rack in aluminum foil-lined roasting pan and place ribs on rack. Brush ribs liberally with sauce. Bake until ribs are tender, about 1 hour and 10 minutes, brushing with more sauce every 20 minutes.

Cut rack into individual ribs or serve in slabs.

BRATS WITH BEER MUSTARD

SERVES 6

❋

IF THE BRATWURST (ALSO KNOWN AS SWISS SAUSAGE) YOU BUY IS UNSMOKED AND UNCURED, BE SURE TO SIMMER IT IN WATER FOR 10 MINUTES BEFORE MARINATING AND BROILING OR GRILLING.

6 to 8 bratwursts

1 can (12 oz) beer

FOR BEER MUSTARD:

6 tablespoons dry mustard

1/2 cup beer

1/2 teaspoon well-drained bottled horseradish

1/4 cup (1/2 stick) butter or margarine

6 to 8 poppy-seed hot dog rolls

6 to 8 pickles

Prick each "brat" 4 times with fork. Place in shallow dish, add beer, and marinate 1 hour.

While brats are marinating, make beer mustard. In small bowl place mustard. Stir in beer and horseradish and let mustard stand at least for 20 minutes before serving.

Preheat broiler. Drain bratwursts. Place on rack on broiler pan and slip into broiler 4 to 6 inches from heat source. Broil until brats begin to brown, 2 to 3 minutes. Turn brats over and continue cooking until skin browns to taste.

While brats are cooking, melt butter in large nonstick skillet over medium heat. Working in batches, place rolls in skillet and brown lightly on both sides.

Place rolls on individual plates with brats. Serve with mustard and pickles.

Note: These sausages also can be grilled over a charcoal fire. Turn them often and grill until the skin begins to "pop."

LAMB SAUSAGES

MAKES 30 SAUSAGES; SERVES 6

❋

THESE TENDER LAMB SAUSAGES ARE SHAPED EASILY AND QUICKLY BY HAND WITHOUT THE USE
OF CASINGS OR A SAUSAGE MAKER.

In food processor fitted with steel blade, combine lamb, pork fat, wine, parsley, rosemary, marjoram, tarragon, nutmeg, and cloves. Pulse machine until ingredients are minced. Shape mixture into pencil-shaped ovals about 1/2 inch by 3 inches.

1 1/2 pounds lean lamb, cut into 3/4-inch pieces
3 ounces pork fat
4 tablespoons dry red wine
3 tablespoons stemmed fresh parsley leaves
1/4 teaspoon each crushed fresh rosemary, dried marjoram, dried tarragon, ground nutmeg, and cloves
2 tablespoons vegetable oil
Tomato Chutney (see page 178)

In nonstick skillet over medium heat, warm oil. Add sausage and fry 2 minutes. Rotate and fry another 2 minutes, or until done.

Serve on warmed platter. Accompany with Tomato Chutney.

LAMB CHOPS WITH HOOSIER MINT ICE

SERVES 6

✺

MINT-FLECKED PURÉED ICE MAKES A REFRESHING COURSE WHEN SERVED JUST AFTER LAMB CHOPS.

FOR MINT ICE:

2 cups superfine sugar

3 1/2 cups water

3/4 cup fresh lemon juice

1 cup minced fresh mint leaves

3 cloves garlic, minced

1/2 teaspoon dried thyme

1/2 teaspoon salt

1/4 teaspoon freshly ground pepper

6 lamb chops (about 6 oz each), trimmed of fat

To make ice, in saucepan stir together sugar and water. Cook over medium heat, stirring occasionally, 6 minutes. Mix in lemon juice.

Place mint leaves in shallow dish and pour hot sugar mixture over top. Cover tightly and place in freezer. Break up ice and purée in food processor fitted with steel blade. Return to freezer.

At mealtime, preheat broiler.

In small bowl, combine garlic, thyme, salt, and pepper. Sprinkle flavoring over both sides of lamb chops.

Arrange chops on rack in broiler pan and slip into broiler about 6 inches from heat source. Broil about 6 minutes, turning after 4 minutes. Cook chops to taste; they are best served slightly pink in the center.

Serve chops on heated platter. Follow with the Mint Ice. Just before serving, purée ice once again and spoon into frosted glasses.

Buffalo Chili

SERVES 6

❋

LOWER IN CALORIES AND FAT THAN OTHER RED MEATS, BUFFALO IS FLAVORFUL AND SATISFYING. WARM TORTILLAS AND A GREEN SALAD ROUND OUT THIS ONE-DISH-MEAL.

In large heavy saucepan over medium heat, fry together bacon and onion, stirring occasionally, until onion is tender, about 5 minutes. Add buffalo meat and brown over medium heat. Stir in all remaining ingredients. Simmer uncovered, stirring occasionally, until buffalo is tender and flavors are blended, about 45 minutes.

Serve hot.

3 slices bacon, cut into 1-inch pieces

1 large onion, minced

2 pounds buffalo, shredded or cut into very small pieces

3 cloves garlic, minced

1 green bell pepper, seeded and sliced

1 can (16 oz) chopped tomatoes with liquid

2 cans (16 oz each) red kidney beans with liquid

2 tablespoons good-quality chili powder

1/2 teaspoon each ground cumin, salt, and celery salt

1/4 teaspoon each hot pepper flakes and dried oregano

1 teaspoon molasses

1 can (6 oz) tomato paste

BUFFALO FOR THE TABLE

Buffalo (or American bison) once roamed the land in such numbers that early explorers couldn't count them. By the 1800s, however, their numbers had been so decimated that the animals were very near extinction. Today, there are more than 60,000 buffalo in both public and private herds, and the demand for buffalo meat is increasing.

A number of better-stocked, upscale supermarkets and gourmet shops offer buffalo, along with other game meats raised for the table, in the frozen food section. Because buffalo raised for market generally is raised similarly to beef cattle, it is likely to be as tender as fine grain-fed lean beef.

Buffalo Steaks with Blackberries

SERVES 4

✳

THIS RECIPE SHOWCASES TWO INGREDIENTS LONG ASSOCIATED WITH THE MIDWEST: BUFFALO (BISON) AND BLACKBERRIES, WHICH, AS THIS RECIPE PROVES, HAVE A NATURAL AFFINITY FOR ONE ANOTHER.

SERVE THESE STEAKS WITH GARLIC MASHED POTATOES (SEE PAGE 103).

4 buffalo steaks (6 to 7 oz each)
Pepper
Garlic powder
3 cups blackberries
1 tablespoon chopped fresh mint
2 tablespoons blackberry brandy

Preheat broiler.

Sprinkle steaks with pepper and garlic powder. Arrange steaks on rack on broiler pan. Slip into broiler 6 inches from heat source. Broil 3 minutes. Turn and broil 2 to 3 minutes longer, or until done to taste. Make small cut in steak to test for doneness.

Meanwhile, in bowl crush 1 cup of the berries. Stir in remaining blackberries, mint, and brandy.

Place steaks on warmed platter. Spoon berry sauce over top. Bring to table piping hot.

GRILLED MEDALLIONS OF VENISON

SERVES 4

❄

ALTHOUGH VENISON REFERS PRIMARILY TO DEER, IT'S A GENERIC TERM FOR MEAT FROM CARI-BOU, MOOSE, ELK, AND ANTELOPE. VENISON-LOVERS FIND ITS FLAVOR REMINISCENT OF FINE AGED LAMB. SERVE THIS FLAVORFUL DISH HOT WITH A CRISP, CHILLED SALAD.

To make marinade, combine all ingredients in small bowl. Pour marinade into large, self-sealing plastic bag. Add venison, seal top securely, and place in bowl. Turn bag several times to make sure all venison has been coated with marinade. Marinate in refrigerator 2 to 4 hours.

Prepare fire in charcoal grill. When coals are ashen, remove venison; discard marinade. Sprinkle venison with seasonings.

FOR MARINADE:

3/4 cup olive oil

1/2 cup dry red wine

2 cloves garlic, minced

1 teaspoon dried tarragon

FOR SEASONINGS:

1 teaspoon garlic powder

2 tablespoons minced dried onion

1/4 teaspoon each hot pepper flakes and chili powder

1/2 teaspoon salt

4 venison medallions (about 4 oz each)

1 red onion, cut crosswise into 4 slices

2 tablespoons olive oil

Put each venison medallion atop an onion slice and place on oiled grill rack or grill screen. Grill 2 minutes. Turn venison and grill 2 minutes longer, or until done to taste. Do not overcook; venison is best when slightly pink on the inside.

Serve immediately.

Venison Kabobs with Pine Nuts

SERVES 4

❋ .

DOUBLE-PRONGED SKEWERS, AN INVALUABLE GRILLING TOOL, HELP KEEP FOOD FROM SLIDING WHEN YOU TURN THE KABOBS. FOR BEST RESULTS, USE A GRILL SCREEN TO PREVENT SMALLER PIECES OF FOOD THREADED ONTO SKEWERS FROM FALLING THROUGH THE GRILL RACK ONTO THE FIRE. ACCOMPANY THESE KABOBS WITH EMBER-COOKED SWEET POTATOES AND STEAMED BROCCOLI.

In bowl stir together all marinade ingredients, then pour into large self-sealing plastic bag. Add venison cubes, seal top securely, and place in shallow bowl. Turn bag several times to make sure all venison has been coated with marinade. Marinate overnight in refrigerator, turning bag once or twice.

FOR TARRAGON MARINADE:

3 cloves garlic, minced

1/4 cup vegetable oil

3/4 cup tarragon vinegar

1/4 teaspoon each chili powder, salt, and pepper

1 1/4 pounds venison loin, cut into 1-inch cubes

16 cherry tomatoes

16 pitted large green olives

16 new potatoes, partially cooked

1/2 cup fresh tarragon leaves, soaked 10 minutes in water to cover and drained

1/2 cup pine nuts

Remove venison from marinade; discard marinade. Using 4 double-pronged skewers, thread on venison cubes, alternating them with tomatoes, olives, and potatoes. Set aside.

Prepare fire in charcoal grill. When coals are ashen, sprinkle tarragon leaves on them. Place skewers on oiled grill rack and grill, rotating every 2 to 3 minutes, until venison is cooked to taste. It tastes best cooked medium-rare to medium; cut into a cube to test for doneness.

Arrange kabobs decoratively on warmed platter. Sprinkle with pine nuts.

CHAPTER 9

On the Side: Vegetables and Side Dishes

Vegetables are part of almost every meal served in restaurants and homes in the Midwest, from hashed brown potatoes at breakfast to corn fritters at lunch to crisp salads at dinner.

The Heartland's primary growing season extends from May through October. All the bounty of the Heartland's agriculture—asparagus, beans, beets, broccoli, brussels sprouts, cabbage, carrots, cauliflower, corn, cucumbers, eggplants, endives, kohlrabi, lettuces, mushrooms, okra, onions, peas, peppers, potatoes, pumpkins, radishes, squashes, tomatoes, turnips, water-cress, and more—can be found in the stalls of the many farmers' markets dotting the urban and rural landscape.

Although midwesterners must rely on other states for year-round access to lettuces and salad greens, they traditionally freeze, can, and otherwise preserve a wealth of other Heartland vegetables. They put up jars of savory relishes, fruit butters, catsups, chutneys, jams, and jellies made from local harvests. Such homemade condiments have long been the hallmark of well-versed midwestern cooks.

Preparing these traditional condiments is easy, but a few tips can make it even simpler. First, do not skimp on the quality of your cookware. A poor-quality, thin-bottomed pan will develop hot spots that could cause burning or scorching. Also, feel free to adjust ingredients to taste. Some preserves can even be made without sugar, although the final product must be processed in a hot-water bath and kept under refrigeration (unlike sugar-laden preserves, which can be stored on a cupboard shelf). And finally, always consult the directions for preserving supplied by the manufacturer of your canning jars and lids.

PLATTER OF PRIMMERS

SERVES 6

✳

THE INTRODUCTION OF A UNIQUE PRODUCT IS ALWAYS CAUSE FOR EXCITEMENT, AND MICHIGAN IS JUSTIFIABLY PROUD OF ITS BABY WHITE ASPARAGUS: THE TINY (ONLY 4 INCHES LONG) IVORY SPEARS OF BABY ASPARAGUS MEASURE A MERE 3/16 TO 1/4 INCH IN DIAMETER AND AVERAGE ABOUT TWO HUNDRED SPEARS TO THE POUND. SHIPPED ALL OVER THE COUNTRY TO RAPIDLY INCREASING NUMBERS OF CUSTOMERS, BABY WHITE ASPARAGUS SPEARS ARE DELICIOUS RAW IN A SALAD OR COOKED ONLY BRIEFLY. HERE, THEY ARE JOINED BY OTHER BABY VEGETABLES. BY THE WAY, A PRIMMER IS ANY YOUNG VEGETABLE HARVESTED EARLY FOR DELICACY OF FLAVOR AND TENDERNESS.

6 cups water

1 tablespoon plus 1 teaspoon salt

1/2 pound baby white asparagus

12 each baby pattypan squash and other mixed baby vegetables such as zucchini, yellow squash, carrots, and green beans

6 tablespoons (3/4 stick) butter or margarine

1/2 teaspoon dried basil

1/2 teaspoon salt

1/4 teaspoon freshly ground pepper

1/2 cup trimmed parsley sprigs

In saucepan bring the water and 1 tablespoon salt to boil. Reduce heat to simmer. Put asparagus and other vegetables in a strainer and lower into water. Blanch 2 minutes, then drain well.

Meanwhile, in small pan melt butter. Arrange drained vegetables decoratively on serving dish. Add basil, salt, and pepper to butter. Stir well and drizzle over vegetables. Garnish with sprigs of parsley. Serve hot.

VEGETABLE SOUFFLÉ
WITH SWEET RED PEPPER SAUCE

SERVES 6

❋

ARNIE MORTON, OF THE POPULAR CHICAGO LANDMARK RESTAURANT, ARNIE'S, HAS BEEN AN INNOVATOR IN THE FIELD OF FINE DINING FOR MANY YEARS. MORTON HAS BEEN A GOOD FRIEND TO THE HEARTLAND FOOD SOCIETY AND TO THE CITY OF CHICAGO.

To make spinach filling, in bowl stir together egg whites, egg yolks, and cream until well blended. In skillet over medium heat, melt butter. Add shallots and sauté until translucent, about 3 minutes. Add spinach and sauté until wilted, about 3 minutes. Remove from heat, drain spinach well and add to cream mixture. Stir in sugar, salt, and pepper. Set aside.

To make tomato filling, in bowl stir together egg whites, egg yolks, and cream

FOR SPINACH FILLING:

3 egg whites

2 egg yolks

3/4 cup whipping cream

2 tablespoons butter

1 teaspoon chopped shallots

10 ounces fresh spinach, washed, drained, and stemmed

1/2 teaspoon sugar

Salt and pepper, to taste

FOR TOMATO FILLING:

3 egg whites

2 egg yolks

3/4 cup whipping cream

1/2 teaspoon minced garlic

1/2 cup minced onion

1 tablespoon tomato paste

1 1/4 cup fresh tomato, peeled, seeded, and diced

1/8 teaspoon sugar

Salt and pepper, to taste

until well blended. In skillet over medium heat, sauté garlic, onion, tomato paste, and diced tomatoes, stirring occasionally, until mixture is thickened. Stir in sugar and salt and pepper. Remove from heat and stir into cream mixture. Set aside.

To make cheese filling, in bowl stir together all ingredients until well blended. Reserve.

Butter a terrine mold and line with parchment paper. Grease parchment. Preheat oven to 350° F.

Place mold in waterbath. Fill mold with spinach mixture.

FOR CHEESE FILLING:

3 egg whites

2 egg yolks

3/4 cup whipping cream

1/3 cup grated Gruyère cheese

1/3 cup freshly grated Parmesan cheese

Salt and pepper, to taste

FOR PEPPER SAUCE:

2 tablespoons (1/4 stick) butter

2 tablespoons diced onion

1/2 cup diced red bell pepper

1/4 cup dry white wine

2 cups half-and-half

Salt and pepper to taste

1/4 cup (1/2 stick) butter

6 fresh button mushrooms

Fresh chives, for garnish

Cook until firm, about 30 minutes; rotate pan after 15 minutes for even cooking. Add tomato mixture to mold (mold should be two-thirds full) and continue cooking until firm, about 1 hour, again rotating every 15 minutes.

Puncture surface of soufflé with tip of knife to release air. Top evenly with cheese mixture (mold should be full at this point). Continue cooking until firm to the touch, about 40 minutes longer. Remove pan from oven and cool 10 minutes. When ready to serve, invert mold onto serving plate and lift off pan. Peel off paper.

While soufflé cooks, make pepper sauce. In saucepan over medium heat, melt 1 tablespoon of the butter. Add onion and bell pepper and sauté until limp but not browned. Stir in wine and reduce over high heat by two thirds. Add half-and-half and reduce by about one half; sauce should be slightly thickened.

Transfer sauce to blender or food processor fitted with steel blade and purée until smooth. Pour purée through fine-mesh sieve and return to clean saucepan.

Return sauce to boil. Season with salt and pepper and swirl in remaining 1 tablespoon butter. Set aside.

In small pan over medium-high heat sauté mushrooms in butter about 1 minute. Pour over finished soufflé and garnish with chopped chives. Serve with pepper sauce.

CANADIAN MAPLE BAKED BEANS

SERVES 8

❋

CANADIAN MAPLE SYRUP FLOWS ABUNDANT DURING LATE WINTER AND EARLY SPRING IN THE CANADIAN CORRIDOR OF THE HEARTLAND. FOLKS SAY THE SUGAR MAPLE TREE GIVES THE SWEETEST SAP, AND BEST OF ALL, TAPPING THE TREE DOES IT NO HARM.

THIS DISH, SWEETENED WITH CANADIAN MAPLE SYRUP, TASTES EVEN BETTER REHEATED THE NEXT DAY.

4 cups navy beans, washed and rinsed

1/3 pound salt pork, cut into 1/2-inch pieces

1 onion, minced

1 teaspoon salt

1/2 teaspoon dry mustard

1/2 teaspoon ground ginger

1/4 cup maple syrup

3 tablespoons catsup

3 tablespoons dark molasses

In large heavy pot place beans. Add water to cover and bring to boil over medium heat. Boil 3 minutes. Remove from heat, cover and let stand 1 1/2 hours. Return to boil, lower heat, and simmer until tender, 45 minutes to 1 hour.

Preheat oven to 325° F.

Transfer beans to ovenproof bean pot or casserole. In skillet over medium heat, fry salt pork and onion 5 minutes. Then stir into bean pot. Stir in salt, mustard, ginger, syrup, catsup, and molasses. Cover bean pot.

Bake beans 3 1/2 to 4 1/2 hours, stirring once each hour. If beans begin to dry out, add water, 1 tablespoon at a time. Serve hot.

MOREL MUSHROOMS

Throughout the Heartland, the coming of spring means the coming of morels, and the intensity of enthusiasm among locals for this fungus is difficult to convey in words.

The thrill of the hunt has to be experienced to be fully appreciated. Morels are mainly "found" or "hunted," and hoarded by their finders. They are only rarely stocked in stores and shops during the season, and then are usually very expensive. Morel hunters regard the discovery of the spongy, honeycombed, cone-shaped cap peeking through the leaves as akin to that of spying a gold nugget in a gold miner's pan.

Although delicate, morels have a distinctive smoky, earthy, nutty flavor that adapts admirably to a legion of dishes. Morels in a cream sauce over homemade pasta is a special favorite. They also give a unique zesty flavor to a green salad and combine delightfully with raw or cooked vegetables. The most popular way to prepare morels, however, is to sauté them, either lightly breaded or fresh from the woods, in butter.

MOREL NOODLES

SERVES 4 TO 6

MORELS MUST ALWAYS BE COOKED BEFORE EATING. BUY THEM FROM REPUTABLE GREEN GRO-
CERS, AND NEVER HUNT THEM YOURSELF UNLESS YOU ARE EXPERIENCED OR ARE WITH A
KNOWLEDGEABLE "HUNTER."

2 large dried morels, washed and soaked 1 hour in water to
   cover, changing water twice

5 eggs

1/2 teaspoon salt

3 to 4 tablespoons extra virgin light olive oil

3 cups flour

FOR SAUCE:

1/4 cup (1/2 stick) butter, cut in 1/2-inch pieces

1 cup small, fresh morel mushrooms, sautéed in
   2 tablespoons butter

1/2 teaspoon dried basil

1/4 teaspoon salt

1/2 cup freshly grated Asiago or Parmesan cheese

Pat drained morels dry with paper towels. Trim stems and place mushrooms in food processor. Purée, then remove from processor and set aside. Combine eggs, salt, and oil in processor bowl. Add flour and mushroom purée. Process until dough gathers around center post, about 20 seconds. Gather dough into a ball and cover lightly. Refrigerate 30 minutes.

Using a pasta machine roll out dough into thin sheets. Cut into 1/2 inch-wide noodles almost 10 inches long. Let dry uncovered.

Bring a large pot filled with salt water to a boil. Add the noodles and cook until al dente, about 4 minutes. Drain and transfer to deep bowl.

Add butter, mushrooms, basil, and salt. Spoon onto dish and sprinkle with cheese.

GRILLED CORN WITH TWO BUTTERS

SERVES 6 TO 8

✳

FRESHLY PICKED EARS OF CORN, GRILLED OVER CHARCOAL IN THEIR HUSKS, ARE ENHANCED BY
TWO BUTTERS—SMOKY BACON AND FRAGRANT WILD ONION. THE ONLY PROBLEM FOR DINERS IS
DECIDING WHICH TO CHOOSE.

12 ears corn

4 slices bacon, cut into 1-inch pieces

1 cup (2 sticks) butter or margarine, or mixture, at room
temperature

1/4 teaspoon hot-pepper flakes

1/4 cup minced wild onion, baby leeks, or green onion

1/4 teaspoon black pepper

2 cups maple wood chips, soaked 30 minutes in water to cover,
and drained

Remove outer husks from corn and discard. Fold back remaining husks and remove silks. Replace husks around ears. Soak corn in water to cover, about 15 minutes.

Prepare fire in charcoal grill. Meanwhile, in heavy skillet over medium heat, fry bacon, stirring often, until crisp. Using slotted spoon remove bacon to paper towels to drain and cool, then crumble into bits. In bowl combine 1/2 cup of the butter, pepper flakes, and bacon bits. Using back of wooden spoon, blend together well. Alternatively, blend ingredients together in food processor fitted with steel blade. Transfer bacon butter to serving bowl and let stand at room temperature.

In bowl combine remaining 1/2 cup butter, wild onion, and black pepper. Using back of wooden spoon blend together well. Alternatively, blend ingredients in food processor fitted with steel blade. Transfer onion butter to serving bowl and let stand at room temperature.

Drain corn. Scatter maple chips over hot coals. Place corn on grill rack and grill, rotating every 3 to 4 minutes, until corn is cooked, 10 to 12 minutes. Husks will char but corn will be done just right. Bring to table hot. Let guests choose their own butter.

CORN FRITTERS

SERVES 6

✳

FRITTERS, FRIED TO A GOLDEN HUE, HAVE A SUCCULENT CORN FLAVOR AND SLIGHTLY CHEWY TEXTURE. COVERED WITH CANADIAN MAPLE SYRUP OR AS AN ACCOMPANIMENT TO MEATS, THEY ARE A TRADITION ON HEARTLAND TABLES.

2 eggs

1/2 cup milk

1 1/3 cups flour

2 tablespoons sugar

1 teaspoon baking powder

1/2 teaspoon salt

3/4 cup canned cream-style corn, drained

2 tablespoons minced red bell pepper

2 to 3 cups canola oil, for frying

Preheat oven to 250° F.

In bowl beat eggs with electric mixer until light. Add in milk, flour, sugar, baking powder, and salt and continue beating until smooth. Using a spoon, stir in corn and red bell pepper.

In large deep sauté or similar pan, pour in oil to depth of 1 inch and heat to 375° F. Scoop up batter by tablespoonfuls and slip into oil, frying only 6 fritters at a time. Fry 1 1/2 minutes, turn fritters, and continue cooking on second side until golden brown, about 1 1/2 minutes longer. Using slotted spoon remove to paper towels to drain briefly. Then transfer to ovenproof platter and place in oven to keep warm until serving. Serve piping hot.

NORWEGIAN POTATO CAKES

MAKES 6 SERVINGS

✳

MRS. CHARLENE KORSLUND, MOTHER OF HEARTLAND FOOD SOCIETY MEMBER DAVID KORSLUND (SEE PAGE VIII), SHARES HER VERSION OF HER FAMILY'S NORWEGIAN POTATO CAKES.

THESE POTATO CAKES ARE A FAVORITE AT THE BAKE SALE AND BAZAAR HELD EACH NOVEMBER BY THE CHURCH SHE ATTENDS. FOR TWO DAYS BEFORE THE SALE, BETWEEN 50 AND 75 WOMEN ALL WORK TOGETHER AT THE CHURCH KITCHEN MAKING OVER 100 DOZEN POTATO CAKES.

MOST FOLKS EAT THEM SPREAD WITH BUTTER AND SUGAR, AND ROLLED UP. THEY ARE ALSO POPULAR WITH BROWN OR CONFECTIONERS' SUGAR.

3 cups cold mashed potatoes

1 cup flour

3/4 teaspoon salt

2 tablespoons butter or margarine, melted, plus extra melted butter for serving

Granulated, brown and/or confectioner's sugar, for serving

In deep bowl mix together potatoes, flour, salt, and butter. Divide mixture in half. On lightly floured board roll out 1/4 to 1/8 inch thick. The pancakes can be cut out in any size desired, from 3- or 5-inch rounds up to the size of a "pan lid cover."

Cook pancakes on hot, ungreased griddle until browned, turning once, about 1 minute on each side. Spread with melted butter and sprinkle with granulated sugar, brown sugar, and/or confectioners' sugar. Serve hot or cold.

POTATO SALAD MILWAUKEE-STYLE

SERVES 8

✳

MOST EVERY FAMILY, INCLUDING YOURS, HAS A FAVORITE POTATO SALAD RECIPE, BUT JUST
ONCE YOU'LL WANT TO TRY THE POTATO SALAD THAT IS FAVORED IN MILWAUKEE.

6 large potatoes, peeled

6 slices bacon, cut into 1-inch pieces

1 red onion, minced

3 celery stalks, diced

1 1/2 tablespoons flour

1/4 cup sugar

1/4 cup minced fresh parsley

1/2 teaspoon salt

1/2 teaspoon celery seed

1/4 teaspoon white pepper

1/2 cup water

1/3 cup cider vinegar

Bring large pot three-fourths full of salted water to boil. Add potatoes and boil until tender when pierced with knife tip, 30 to 45 minutes. Drain, cool, and cut into dice. Place potatoes in bowl. Set aside.

In large heavy skillet over medium heat, fry bacon, stirring often, until crisp. Drain on paper towels. Add onion and celery to bacon drippings in skillet and sauté over medium heat, stirring occasionally, until tender, about 5 minutes. Whisk in flour, sugar, parsley, salt, celery seed, and pepper and cook 1 minute over medium heat. Stir in water and vinegar and boil 1 minute. Add bacon pieces and potatoes and toss ingredients together until heated through.

Place in serving bowl and serve hot.

WILD RICE

The only grain truly native to the Midwest is wild rice, an aquatic grass. It flourishes in the lakes and rivers of the Heartland. The Menominees even took their name from the Indian word for wild rice, mahnomen.

In the past, both the Ojibway and Menominee tribes harvested wild rice by canoe, starting in late August and continuing into the fall. Indian women, two to a boat, paddled out onto the water. One woman paddled as the other stroked the fronds between two wooden sticks, shucking the mature grain into the bottom of the boat. The immature seeds remained on the fronds until ready for harvesting.

Today, canoe harvesting of wild rice continues, although "lake rice," as the product is called, accounts for just 15 percent of the total crop. The bulk of today's crop has been hybridized for mechanized paddy farming. Paddy rice matures evenly and the grains are harder and darker in color than the natural wild rice harvested by hand. The flavor, however, is similar.

WILD ONIONS WITH WILD RICE

SERVES 6

❋

THE INDIAN WORD CHE-CA-GOU, BECAME CHICAGO. IT MEANS "GREAT" OR "POWERFUL."
ILLINOIS INDIANS ALSO USED THIS WORD TO REFER TO THE WILD ONIONS AND THE LAND ON
WHICH THEY GREW IN ABUN-
DANCE. WILD ONIONS ARE DIF-
FICULT TO OBTAIN COMMER-
CIALLY AND CANNOT BE
DOMESTICATED. THEY HAVE A
MILD, FRAGRANT TASTE AND
RESEMBLE YOUNG LEEKS
(WHICH CAN BE SUBSTITUTED
FOR THEM).

4 cups water

1 teaspoon salt

1 cup wild rice, washed and drained

6 tablespoons (3/4 stick) butter or margarine

2 cloves garlic, minced

4 shallots, minced

1/4 cup chopped wild onion or young leek

1/4 teaspoon salt

1/4 teaspoon pepper

1/4 cup minced fresh parsley

Bring water to boil, add salt, and slowly stir in rice. Cook without stirring until tender, or about 40 minutes, covered.

In medium to heavy frying pan over medium heat, melt butter. Add garlic, shallots, and wild onion and sauté, stirring occasionally, until tender, about 4 minutes. Mix in salt, pepper, and parsley.

Toss onion mixture with rice and serve hot.

SPAETZLE

SERVES 6 TO 8

✸

SPAETZLE CAME WITH GERMAN IMMIGRANTS TO THE HEARTLAND. DELICATE, LIGHT EGG DUMPLINGS, THEY ARE A FESTIVE ACCOMPANIMENT TO ROAST MEATS (ESPECIALLY VEAL), OR BROTH OR SOUP. THEY ALSO MAKE A SATISFYING SIDE DISH TOSSED WITH BUTTER AND MINCED PARSLEY.

2 cups flour

2 eggs

1 1/2 teaspoons salt

1/2 teaspoon white pepper

1 cup milk

In deep mixing bowl combine flour, eggs, 1/2 teaspoon of the salt and pepper. Slowly stir in milk, then whisk until batter is smooth. Let stand 15 minutes, then stir again.

Bring a large pot filled with water to a rolling boil over medium-high heat. Add remaining salt. Spoon a few tablespoonfuls of batter into a spaetzle maker or large-holed colander and, holding it over the boiling water, pour batter through spaetzle maker or colander into water. Repeat until all batter is in the water.

Boil spaetzle rapidly until cooked, 6 to 8 minutes. They should have a soft, doughlike texture.

Drain spaetzle and serve.

STEAMED FIDDLEHEADS

SERVES 6

✹

STARTING IN MAY, THE FIDDLEHEAD FERN, WITH ITS GRACEFULLY COILED FRONDS, CRUNCHY TEXTURE, AND UNIQUE FLAVOR, BECOMES THE PREMIUM VEGETABLE IN MICHIGAN FOR FORAGING. THIS VERSATILE PLANT CAN BE STEAMED, MARINATED, OR EATEN RAW. ITS EXQUISITE FORM WILL AROUSE CURIOSITY AMONG THE UNINITIATED, AND ITS VERSATILITY AND FLAVOR MAKE IT A WELCOME SPRINGTIME ARRIVAL.

HARVEST ONLY FROM PLENTIFUL SITES, AND SELECT TIGHTLY CURLED SHOOTS.

1 pound fiddlehead ferns, washed
3 tablespoons extra virgin olive oil
1 1/2 tablespoons balsamic vinegar
Salt and pepper, to taste

Arrange fiddlehead ferns on steamer rack over boiling water. Cover and steam until tender, about 7 minutes.

Place ferns in bowl and toss with olive oil and vinegar. Season with salt and pepper and serve.

SALAD OF GREENS AND MAYTAG BLUE CHEESE

SERVES 6

✳

IN ADDITION TO PRODUCING A FAMOUS WASHING MACHINE, THE MAYTAG FAMILY OF NEWTON, IOWA, HAS A PRIZED HERD OF HOLSTEIN CATTLE, THE SOURCE OF THE MILK FOR THEIR BLUE CHEESE. IN 1941, THE MAYTAGS BEGAN TO MANUFACTURE FINE CHEESE AND SELL IT BY MAIL ORDER. TODAY, 80 PERCENT OF THIS WONDERFUL CHEESE IS STILL SOLD THROUGH THE MAIL.

1 head romaine lettuce, torn into bite-size pieces

1 head Belgian endive, sliced crosswise into 1/2-inch thick pieces

3 green onions, minced

1 cup shredded smoked turkey or chicken (optional)

FOR DRESSING:

1/2 cup tarragon vinegar

3/4 teaspoon prepared mustard

2 cloves garlic, minced

1/3 cup extra virgin olive oil

Salt and pepper, to taste

1 cup crumbled Maytag blue cheese

2 Red Delicious apples, cored, and chopped

1/2 cup chopped walnuts

Place lettuce and endive in salad bowl. Top with onions and turkey. Set aside.

To make dressing, in small bowl whisk together vinegar, mustard, and garlic. Whisk in oil until well blended. Season with salt and pepper.

Pour dressing over salad and toss well. Sprinkle with cheese, apples and nuts. Bring to the table and toss again before serving. Serve on chilled salad plates.

PICKLED LEEKS

SERVES 6 TO 8

TANTALIZING US WITH THEIR WONDERFUL ONION-GARLIC FLAVOR AND HEADY AROMA, LEEKS ARE DELICIOUS FINELY CUT IN SALADS, GRILLED OR SAUTÉED WHOLE, OR IN SOUPS AND STEWS. PICKLED LEEKS, AS PREPARED BY THE ROWE INN, MICHIGAN, ARE A GREAT ACCOMPANIMENT FOR PÂTÉ OR GRILLED SAUSAGE. THIS RECIPE REQUIRES A BIT OF PREPARATION, BUT THE RESULTS ARE WELL WORTH THE EFFORT.

2 pounds wild leeks (or young, thin leeks), roots removed and leeks trimmed to 1 1/2 to 2 inches

Boiling water, as needed

3/4 cup kosher salt

4 cups water

4 cups white vinegar

2 cups sugar

2 tablespoons hot pepper flakes

5 bay leaves

10 whole cloves

2 tablespoons each dried dill and whole peppercorns

Place leeks in bowl and add boiling water to cover. Drain and remove outside layer of leeks.

In bowl combine salt and the water, stirring to dissolve salt. Add leeks; they should be completely submerged. Cover and refrigerate 2 days. Drain and rinse well under cold running water. Drain again and place in deep bowl.

In saucepan combine vinegar, sugar, pepper flakes, bay leaves, cloves, dill, and peppercorns. Bring to boil. Pour over the leeks, cover, and refrigerate.

Leeks will keep 2 months in refrigerator. For longer storage, spoon into hot, sterilized jars and process 30 minutes in hot-water bath, or according to manufacturer's directions.

PICKLED CRAB APPLES

SERVES 8

✳

CRAB APPLES ARE AVAILABLE IN
THE HEARTLAND IN AUGUST
AND SEPTEMBER. THEY ARE A
DELECTABLE COMPLEMENT TO
MEATS AND POULTRY.

2 1/2 pounds crab apples

1 cup sugar

1/4 teaspoon ground cloves

1 tablespoon ground cinnamon

1/2 teaspoon ground nutmeg

3/4 cup cider vinegar

Preheat oven to 325° F.

Arrange apples in heavy baking pan, stem side up. Set aside.

In small heavy saucepan combine all remaining ingredients. Bring to boil over medium heat, stirring to dissolve sugar. Remove from heat and cool 5 minutes. Pour sugar mixture over apples. Cover and bake 2 hours. Cool. Transfer to deep bowl, cover, and refrigerate.

SWEET ONION JELLY

MAKES ABOUT 2 CUPS

TRY UNUSUAL ONION JELLY WITH TURKEY OR DUCK. FOR MAXIMUM FLAVOR, SERVE WARM OR AT ROOM TEMPERATURE, RATHER THAN CHILLED.

1/4 cup (1/2 stick) butter or margarine
2 1/2 cups thinly sliced white onions
1/3 cup sugar
1/4 cup white wine vinegar
1/4 teaspoon white pepper
1/2 cup chopped dried apricots
3/4 cup dry white wine

In medium to heavy saucepan over medium heat, melt butter. Add onions, sauté, stirring often, until softened, about 4 minutes.

Add all remaining ingredients, reduce heat to low and simmer, stirring often, for 10 minutes.

Continue simmering for 10 minutes more. Cool.

Spoon onion jelly into serving bowl. Cover lightly and refrigerate until ready to serve.

APPLE BUTTER

MAKES ABOUT 5 CUPS

✻

MAKING UP A BATCH OF SPICY APPLE BUTTER IS SUCH A LONG-STANDING CUSTOM IN THE HEARTLAND THAT AN AMPLE KETTLE TO COOK IT IN IS A FAMILY TREASURE, HANDED DOWN FROM ONE GENERATION TO THE NEXT. TRY IT ON THICK SLICES OF HOMEMADE BREAD OR TOAST. HIGHLY FLAVORED APPLES SUCH AS JONATHANS OR WINESAPS ARE ESPECIALLY GOOD IN THIS RECIPE.

3 pounds tart cooking apples, peeled, cored, and sliced

1 cup apple juice

2 1/4 cups sugar

2 tablespoons ground cinnamon

1/2 teaspoon ground nutmeg

1/2 teaspoon ground cloves

1 teaspoon vanilla extract

1/4 cup (1/2 stick) butter

In heavy saucepan toss together all ingredients. Simmer uncovered over medium-low heat, stirring occasionally, until apples are soft, about 45 minutes. Remove mixture to bowl. Mash apples and return mixture to pan. Continue simmering until mixture is smooth, about 45 minutes.

Ladle into hot, sterilized jars and seal according to manufacturer's directions.

PEACH BUTTER

MAKES 2 TO 3 CUPS

✳

USING BOTTLED OR CANNED NECTAR INTENSIFIES THE PEACH FLAVOR OF THIS FRUIT BUTTER.

4 cans (16 oz each) peaches, drained

2 cans (12 oz each) peach nectar

1 teaspoon ground cinnamon

1 1/2 cups brown sugar

1/4 teaspoon ground nutmeg

In food processor fitted with steel blade or in blender, purée peaches.

Transfer to large heavy saucepan. Stir in nectar, cinnamon, sugar, and nutmeg. Bring to boil. Reduce heat to simmer and continue cooking, stirring often until thick, about 1 hour and 45 minutes. Cool.

Pour into jar. Cover tightly and refrigerate.

STATE FAIRS

Midwestern state fairs promote local industry, livestock, history, and spirit. The Michigan State Fair includes a display of antique automobiles, in homage to the manufacturers of the Motor City, Detroit. The Indiana State Fair hosts many family activities to educate children in Hoosier history. And the Wisconsin State Fair sponsors a special cheese-carving contest, in acknowledgment of the state's dairy industry. Displays of cattle and hogs are a high point of the Iowa State Fair. And events at the Illinois State Fair run the gamut from art fairs to pie baking contests.

Foodstuffs commonly exhibited at state fairs include homemade pies, cakes, cookies, candies, breads, sausages, specialty meats, jams, jellies, preserves, pickles, and canned fruits and vegetables. Judges sample the wares of the finest home cooks in the state and award blue, red, and yellow ribbons. Several blue-ribbon recipes have been used as a launching pad for cottage industries. Gourmet food companies wisely market their prize-winning dill pickled green beans or strawberry-rhubarb preserves with the state fair blue-ribbon seal displayed on the label.

STATE FAIR STRAWBERRY JAM

MAKES ABOUT 3 CUPS

✳

THE SIMPLEST INGREDIENTS—SWEET STRAWBERRIES, PICKED AT THEIR PEAK OF RIPENESS, AND
SUGAR—MAKE THIS JAM A BLUE-RIBBON WINNER.

4 cups hulled strawberries

4 cups sugar

Place 2 cups of the strawberries in blender or in food processor fitted with steel blade and purée. Transfer to heavy saucepan and add 2 cups of the sugar. Bring to boil over medium heat. Cook uncovered, stirring occasionally with wooden spoon, 10 minutes.

Add remaining 2 cups whole berries and 2 cups sugar. Continue boiling over medium heat, stirring occasionally, for 8 to 10 minutes. Immediately pour into bowl. Cool completely, stirring often. Cover and refrigerate.

Ladle into hot, sterilized jars and seal according to manufacturer's directions.

PLUM CATSUP

MAKES 2 1/2 TO 3 CUPS

✹

EVEN DISDAINERS OF TOMATO CATSUP WILL ENJOY THE SWEET-SOUR GOODNESS OF THIS CONDIMENT.

2 cups fresh purple plums, halved, and pitted, or 32 canned plums, halved and pitted, with liquid
1 onion, minced
1 cup cider vinegar
1 cup sugar
1/2 teaspoon each salt, dry mustard, and ground cinnamon
1/4 teaspoon each pepper and ground cloves

In saucepan combine plums and onion. Add water to cover (or juice from canned plums, if using). Bring to boil over medium heat. Reduce heat to low and simmer until tender, 20 to 25 minutes if using fresh fruit, or 10 minutes for canned.

Drain plums and place in food processor fitted with steel blade or blender. Purée.

Return purée to clean pan. Stir in vinegar, sugar, salt, mustard, cinnamon, pepper, and cloves. Bring mixture to boil. Reduce heat to low and simmer uncovered for 20 minutes.

Cool, place in bottle, and cover tightly. Refrigerate.

SPICY PUMPKIN CATSUP

MAKES ABOUT 2 1/2 CUPS

※

THE HEARTLAND SPA (SEE PAGE 209) RECOMMENDS SERVING THIS CATSUP WITH HOT OR COLD TURKEY.

In saucepan combine all ingredients and stir well. Place over medium-low heat and simmer about 1 hour. Transfer to food processor fitted with steel blade. Purée.

1 can (16 oz) pumpkin purée

1 onion, chopped finely

1 apple or pear, cored and chopped

1/2 cup cider vinegar

1 cup water

2 1/2 tablespoons honey

1/2 teaspoon each ground cloves, curry powder, ground all-spice, cayenne, salt

Freshly ground pepper, to taste

Serve at once, or cool in cold-water bath, cover, and store in refrigerator.

INDIANA RED TOMATO CHUTNEY

MAKES 7 CUPS

✳

DELICIOUS WITH LAMB SAUSAGES (SEE PAGE 144) AND OTHER SAVORY FOODS, THIS TOMATO CHUTNEY MAKES A FINE GIFT FOR PRESENTING TO YOUR HOST OR HOSTESS.

Combine chopped tomatoes, carrots, apples, celery, lime juice, cloves, ginger, vinegar, brown sugar, raisins, parsley, cinnamon, and ground cloves, nutmeg, and allspice in a large heavy saucepan. Bring mixture to a boil. Reduce heat to simmer and cook uncovered, stirring frequently, for 1 1/2 hours, or until chutney is thick.

Cool chutney. Place in a deep bowl, cover, and refrigerate. Store for later use.

6 large tomatoes, peeled, and chopped

2 medium carrots, grated

3 large Golden Delicious apples, peeled and chopped

2 stalks celery, chopped

4 tablespoons freshly squeezed lime juice

3 whole cloves

2 slices candied ginger, chopped

1 cup cider vinegar

1 cup firmly packed, light brown sugar

1/4 cup raisins

4 tablespoons chopped parsley

1/2 teaspoon ground cinnamon

1/4 teaspoon each ground cloves, ground nutmeg, and ground allspice

TOMATO HOT SAUCE

MAKES ABOUT 2 CUPS

❋

NOT YOUR AVERAGE TOMATO SAUCE, THIS ONE IS HEATED UP WITH HORSERADISH FROM THE HORSERADISH CAPITAL OF THE WORLD, A TWO-COUNTY AREA AROUND COLLINSVILLE, ILLINOIS. THIS AREA IS RESPONSIBLE FOR 75 PERCENT OF THE WORLD'S HORSERADISH PRODUCTION.

COLLINSVILLE HORSERADISH HAS THE BEST QUALITY AND THE HIGHEST PUNGENCY OF ANY COMMERCIALLY GROWN HORSERADISH IN THE UNITED STATES. AUTHORITIES ATTRIBUTE THESE SUPERLATIVES TO THE AREA'S LONG GROWING SEASON AND THE HIGH MINERAL CONTENT OF ITS SOIL.

8 tomatoes

1 onion, minced

1 green bell pepper, seeded and chopped

3 tablespoons firmly packed dark brown sugar

1/2 teaspoon salt

2 teaspoons well-drained bottled horseradish

2 1/2 teaspoons pickling spices

Quarter tomatoes and remove seeds. Place in food processor fitted with steel blade and purée.

Transfer to saucepan. Add onion, bell pepper, sugar, salt, and horseradish. Tie pickling spices in cheesecloth bag and add to pan. Bring to boil over medium heat. Reduce heat to low simmer, cover partially and simmer 8 to 10 minutes.

Remove pickling spice bag. Transfer to bowl, cover and refrigerate. Stir well before serving.

HOT BRANDIED APPLESAUCE

MAKES 3 TO 4 CUPS

＊

THE ADDITION OF APPLEJACK, A BRANDY MADE FROM THE BOUNTIFUL APPLE CROPS OF THE MIDWEST, GIVES THIS APPLE-SAUCE A SURPRISING TANG.

2 pounds apples (7 or 8 large apples), peeled, cored, and sliced

1 cup sugar

3/4 cup water

1 tablespoon grated lemon zest

1 teaspoon ground cinnamon

1/4 teaspoon ground nutmeg

1/4 cup applejack or other brandy

In saucepan combine apples, sugar, water, lemon zest, cinnamon, and nutmeg. Simmer uncovered over medium-low heat, stirring often, until apples are tender, or about 35 minutes.

Mash with potato masher. Stir in brandy. Reheat slightly before serving.

CHAPTER 10

Heartland Desserts

Throughout the Midwest, desserts are as much a part of the meal as the main dish, and baked goods come from the heart as well as the Heartland. Midwestern culinary traditions parallel the ethnic and religious cultures of the regions in which their immigrant ancestors settled. Desserts also are a hallmark of the cook's expertise in transforming local ingredients into pies, cakes, cookies, and other sweet endings to a memorable midwestern meal.

CAPPUCCINO COOKIES

MAKES 8 DOZEN

✳

THE CONTRIBUTOR OF THIS SOPHISTICATED COOKIE RECIPE, DAVID RADWINE, FORMER CHEF OF THE MIDLAND HOTEL, CHICAGO, HOSTED A BRUNCH FOR THE FIRST HEARTLAND FOOD SOCIETY SEMINAR. RADWINE CURRENTLY MANAGES THE SANGAMO CLUB IN SPRINGFIELD, ILLINOIS.

8 ounces semisweet chocolate

2 cups (4 sticks) butter, at room temperature

1 cup each granulated sugar and firmly packed brown sugar

2 eggs

2 tablespoons instant coffee, dissolved in 2 tablespoons hot water

4 cups flour

2 teaspoons ground cinnamon

1/4 teaspoon salt

In top pan of double boiler over hot water, melt 4 ounces of the chocolate. Set aside to cool.

In bowl and using electric mixer, cream together butter, granulated sugar, brown sugar, and eggs until light and fluffy. Add diluted coffee and chocolate and beat until incorporated.

In bowl sift together flour, cinnamon, and salt. Add to creamed mixture and beat well. Cover and chill batter at least 1 hour. Shape batter into logs 1 inch in diameter. Cover with plastic wrap and chill 24 hours before baking.

Preheat oven to 300° F.

When ready to bake, cut logs into 1/4-inch-thick slices. Arrange on nonstick baking sheets. Bake 8 to 10 minutes.

When cookies are cool, melt remaining chocolate. Using a spoon drizzle chocolate decoratively over cookies. When chocolate hardens, cookies are ready to serve.

COMMUNITY CUISINES

Religious persecution was one of the primary forces motivating immigrants to seek newer and safer places to live and worship. The Midwest proved to be a haven to groups such as the Amana, Amish, and Mennonites.

The Amana colonies, originated in Germany in the sixteenth century. In 1843, Amana leader Christian Mets settled in Buffalo, New York. By 1855, "go west" fervor was strong enough to persuade Mets and several others to relocate. They chose a fertile, 25,000-acre area along the banks of the Iowa River, where their descendents continue to live according to cooperative principles, emphasizing communal property and agriculture. Old World German sausages, cheeses, and breads are among Amana society specialities.

In addition to settlements in Lancaster County, Pennsylvania, pockets of Amish and Mennonite settlers exist in Wisconsin, Michigan, and Indiana.

The Mennonite sect was formed in Switzerland in 1525. The Amish are a more conservative splinter group of the Mennonite church, believing in utter simplicity of dress and life-style, and work. For example, Mennonite cooks use frozen foods, salad dressings, and canned goods in cooking. Strict Amish cooks, however, never use commercial goods, preferring to work with natural ingredients.

Today, many of these communities can be visited, such as the Amana colonies in Iowa and the Amish towns of Middlebury and New Harmony, Indiana, and Bishop Hill, Illinois. There are bed-and-breakfasts, country inns, and, of course, a number of wonderful restaurants.

ILLINOIS AMISH WHOOPIE COOKIES

MAKES 6 DOZEN SINGLE COOKIES, OR 3 DOZEN SANDWICH COOKIES

✹

THESE OATMEAL COOKIES ARE GOOD BY THEMSELVES, AND EVEN BETTER WHEN MADE AS A SANDWICH COOKIE WITH CREAMY FILLING.

l 1/2 cups (3 sticks) margarine, at room temperature

4 cups firmly packed light brown sugar

4 eggs

4 1/2 cups flour

2 teaspoons ground cinnamon

2 teaspoons baking powder

1 teaspoon salt

4 cups rolled oats

4 teaspoons baking soda

FOR FILLING:

2 medium egg whites

3/4 cup vegetable shortening

1 1/2 tablespoons flour

1 1/2 teaspoons vanilla extract

l 1/2 tablespoons milk

2 cups confectioner's sugar

Preheat oven to 350° F. Lightly grease baking sheet.

In large bowl and using electric mixer, cream together margarine and brown sugar. Add eggs, one at a time, and beat until incorporated.

In deep bowl sift together flour, cinnamon, baking powder, and salt. Add flour mixture to butter mixture and beat until incorporated. Add rolled oats and baking soda and again beat until thoroughly incorporated.

Drop batter by heaping tablespoonfuls, 2 inches apart, onto prepared baking sheet. Bake until firm to the touch and golden brown, 15 to 20 minutes. Cool on pan 5 minutes, then remove to rack to cool.

While cookies are baking, make filling. Place egg whites in large bowl and beat lightly with electric mixer. Add vegetable shortening and beat together until combined. Add flour, vanilla, milk, and confectioner's sugar and continue beating until batter is consistency of frosting.

To assemble, spread 2 teaspoons filling, or to taste, on bottom of half of cooled cookies. Gently top with second cookie, bottom down. Chill until ready to serve.

DODD'S BUTTERMILK PIE

SERVES 6

❋

FOUR GENERATIONS OF THE DODD FAMILY HAVE BEEN IN THE RESTAURANT BUSINESS IN INDIANAPOLIS SINCE 1942. THE CULINARY TRADITIONS OF DODD'S TOWNHOUSE ARE AS ROOTED IN THE REGION'S HISTORY AS THE 1900 LOG CABIN THAT HOUSES THE RESTAURANT.

THE PIE FILLING CAN BE MADE WITH AN ELECTRIC MIXER OR BY HAND. IF USING A MIXER, HOWEVER, DO NOT RUN IT ON HIGH SPEED AS IT WILL BEAT TOO MUCH AIR INTO THE PIE FILLING.

3 eggs
3/4 cup sugar
1/4 cup plus flour
1 teaspoon vanilla extract
1 cup buttermilk
1/4 cup (1 stick) tablespoons butter, melted and cooled
9-inch unbaked pie shell (or use 1/2 recipe for pie pastry on page 186)

Preheat oven to 375° F.

In mixing bowl beat together eggs and sugar. Stir in flour. In separate bowl beat together vanilla, buttermilk, and butter. Mix into egg mixture.

Pour filling into pie shell. Bake until pie tests done, (until knife inserted in center comes out clean) about 45 minutes. Remove to rack to cool, then slice and serve.

TART CHERRY PIE

SERVES 6 TO 8

❋

FRESH TART, OR SOUR, CHERRIES SUCH AS THOSE GROWN ALONG THE MICHIGAN SHORELINE OF THE GREAT LAKES SHOULD BE BRIGHT AND GLOSSY, WITH FRESH-LOOKING STEMS. A CHERRY PITTER, A KITCHEN TOOL THAT RESEMBLES A HOLE PUNCHER, MAKES RELATIVELY QUICK WORK OF REMOVING THE PITS.

TART CHERRY PIE IS A TRADITIONAL ACCOMPANIMENT TO THE HEARTLAND FISH FRY (SEE PAGE 106).

FOR PIE PASTRY:

2 1/4 cups flour

1/2 teaspoon salt

2/3 cup vegetable shortening

2 tablespoons butter

About 7 tablespoons ice water

FOR FILLING:

5 cups pitted tart cherries

3 tablespoons instant tapioca

1 cup sugar

1/4 teaspoon ground mace

1/4 teaspoon ground cardamom

2 tablespoons butter or butter blend, cut into small pieces

FOR TOPPING:

2 tablespoons milk

Sugar, for sprinkling

Preheat oven to 375° F.

To make pastry, combine flour, salt, shortening, and butter in food processor fitted with steel blade. Process briefly until mixture has crumbly texture. With machine running, add water through tube and process until dough ball forms around center post, 45 to 60 seconds. Gather dough into ball, wrap in plastic wrap, and refrigerate 30 to 35 minutes.

Alternatively, in large bowl stir together flour and salt. Using pastry blender or 2 knives cut in shortening and butter until mixture has crumbly texture. Sprinkle water over mixture and stir with fork until smooth dough forms. Gather into ball, wrap and refrigerate. Divide dough in half. On lightly floured board roll out half of dough into round large enough to line plate. Reserve remaining dough for top of pie.

To make filling, in large bowl gently toss together cherries, tapioca, sugar, mace, and cardamom. Mound filling in pastry-lined plate. Sprinkle with butter pieces.

On lightly floured surface roll out remaining pastry into round large enough to cover pie comfortably. Set crust in place, trim away any excess pastry, and crimp edges. Cut several 1/2-inch vents in top. Brush top with milk. Sprinkle lightly with sugar.

Bake pie on center oven rack until crust is golden color, 55 to 60 minutes. Cool on rack. Best served warm.

SHOO-FLY PIE

SERVES 6

❋

THIS HEARTLAND VERSION OF A PENNSYLVANIA DUTCH FAVORITE IS BEST SERVED WARM.

To make pastry, combine flour, salt, shortening, and butter in food processor fitted with steel blade. Process briefly until mixture has crumbly texture. With machine running, add the ice water through feed tube and process until doughball forms around center post, 6 or 7 seconds. Add more ice water by the tablespoon if necessary. Dough should be soft and workable. Gather dough into ball, wrap in aluminum foil and refrigerate 30 minutes.

Alternatively, in large

FOR PASTRY:

1 1/2 cups flour

1/2 teaspoon salt

3 tablespoons vegetable shortening

6 tablespoons (3/4 stick) unsalted butter

4 to 5 tablespoons ice water

FOR FILLING:

1/2 teaspoon baking soda

1 cup warm water

1 egg

1/4 cup firmly packed dark brown sugar

1/8 teaspoon each ground cinnamon and cloves

1 tablespoon flour

1/2 cup light corn syrup

FOR CRUMB TOPPING:

1/2 cup flour

1/4 cup firmly packed light brown sugar

1/4 teaspoon baking powder

*1/8 teaspoon each salt and ground nutmeg, ginger, and
    cinnamon*

*2 tablespoons vegetable shortening, butter, or margarine, at
    room temperature*

bowl stir together flour and salt. Using pastry blender or 2 knives cut in butter and shortening until mixture has crumbly texture. Sprinkle the water over mixture and stir with fork until soft,

FOR GINGER WHIPPED CREAM:

1 cup whipping cream, chilled

1/2 teaspoon each ground ginger, cinnamon, and vanilla extract

3 tablespoons minced candied ginger

1/4 cup sugar

smooth dough forms. Gather into ball, wrap, and refrigerate.

On lightly floured board roll out dough into round large enough to line 9-inch pie plate. Fit into pie plate and crimp edges.

Preheat oven to 350° F.

To make filling, in mixing bowl dissolve baking soda in the water. Stir in egg, sugar, cinnamon, cloves, flour, and corn syrup until incorporated. Pour into pie shell.

To make topping, in bowl mix together flour, sugar, baking powder, salt, nutmeg, ginger, and cinnamon. Using fork, mix in shortening, working it in until crumbly consistency forms. Sprinkle crumb mixture over filling. Do not mix in.

Bake until knife inserted in center comes out clean, about 55 minutes. Cover crust with aluminum foil if it begins to brown. Cool on wire rack.

Just before serving make whipped cream. In chilled bowl and with electric mixer, beat cream until soft peaks form. Sprinkle with ginger, cinnamon, and vanilla and beat 1 minute. Sprinkle with candied ginger and sugar, mix in and continue beating until stiff peaks form, 1 to 2 minutes longer. Top pie with whipped cream and serve.

Three-Layer Carrot Cake with Black Walnut Frosting

SERVES 10-12

❋

THIS RICH, MOIST, CAKE FREEZES WELL AND IS EXCELLENT FOR BUFFET-STYLE DINING.

Preheat oven to 350° F.

Grease three 8-inch cake pans. In large bowl using electric mixer, beat butter until light. Beat in eggs and sugar and continue beating until light. In separate bowl stir together flour, cinnamon, nutmeg, cloves, baking powder, and salt. Add to egg mixture alternately with raisins, apricots, and carrots.

Spoon batter into prepared pans, dividing it evenly among them. Bake until tester inserted in center of cakes comes out clean, about

1/2 cup (1 stick) butter or margarine, at room temperature cut into 1/2-inch pieces

4 eggs

1 3/4 cups sugar

1 1/2 cups flour

1 1/2 teaspoon ground cinnamon

1/4 teaspoon each ground nutmeg and cloves

1 1/4 baking powder

1/2 teaspoon salt

1/2 cup raisins

1/2 cup dried apricots or cranberries

3 cups grated carrots

FOR FROSTING:

8 ounces cream cheese, at room temperature, cut into small pieces

6 tablespoons (3/4 stick) butter or margarine, at room temperature

3 1/2 to 4 cups confectioner's sugar, sifted

1 teaspoon vanilla extract

1 cup black walnuts, chopped

30 minutes. Cool in pans for 10 minutes. Invert onto racks and cool completely.

To prepare frosting, in large bowl, beat cream cheese until light, then beat in butter. Add sugar, 1 cup at a time, and beat until smooth. Add only as much sugar as is necessary to make spreadable consistency. Mix in vanilla and walnuts.

To assemble, place 1 cake layer on serving plate. Frost sides and top. Top with another layer; again frost sides and top. Repeat again with third layer. Refrigerate until ready to serve.

MALTED MILK CANDY CAKE

SERVES 8

❋

THIS RICH LAYER CAKE LACED WITH ROUGHLY GROUND MALTED MILK BALLS CELEBRATES CHICAGO'S CLAIM THAT IT IS THE NATION'S CANDY CAPITAL.

Preheat oven to 350° F. Grease three 8-inch cake pans.

In large bowl and using electric mixer, cream together butter and sugar until light and fluffy. Add eggs, oil, and cocoa and beat in until incorporated.

In another bowl sift together flour, baking powder, baking soda, and salt. Add to egg mixture alternately with buttermilk and sour cream. Mix in vanilla and malted milk balls.

Spoon batter into pans, dividing it evenly among them. Bake until tester inserted in center of cake comes out clean, about 25 minutes. Cool in pan 5 minutes,

1/4 cup (1/2 stick) butter, at room temperature

1 1/4 cups sugar

2 eggs

1/2 cup vegetable oil

1/2 cup powdered cocoa

2 cups cake flour

1 1/4 teaspoons baking soda

1/4 teaspoon baking powder

1/4 teaspoon salt

Scant 1 cup buttermilk

1/2 cup sour cream

1 teaspoon vanilla extract

1 cup malted milk balls, roughly ground

FOR FROSTING:

1/2 cup (1 stick) butter or margarine

1/2 cup powdered cocoa

4 cups confectioner's sugar, or as needed, sifted

1/2 cup half-and-half, or as needed

1 1/2 teaspoons vanilla extract

then cool completely on wire rack. Brush off any crumbs before frosting.

To make frosting, in saucepan over medium heat, combine butter and cocoa and, stirring often, bring to boil. Pour into large bowl. Stir in sugar alternately with half-and-half. Mix in vanilla. Mixture should be frosting consistency. If too thick add more half-and-half, a tablespoon at a time; if too thin, beat in more sifted confectioner's sugar, by the 1/4 cup at a time.

Frost top and sides of cooled cake.

JEAN BANCHET CHOCOLATE CAKE

SERVES 8

✻

HOW LUCKY FOR THE HEARTLAND TO HAVE JEAN BANCHET AND HIS CHARMING WIFE, DORIS, SETTLE HERE MORE THAN TWENTY YEARS AGO. THE BANCHETS FOUNDED THE INTERNATIONAL-LY ACCLAIMED LE FRANÇAIS IN WHEELING, ILLINOIS, WHICH THEY HAVE SINCE SOLD. THE RESTAURANT SET THE TONE FOR FINE DINING IN THE MIDWEST. THE GANACHE (FROSTING), AN ELEGANT CREAMY TOPPING THAT IS SIMPLE TO MAKE, IS EVIDENCE OF THEIR REMARK-ABLE STYLE.

6 eggs, separated

3/4 cup sugar

2 tablespoons powdered cocoa, sifted

1/4 cup flour, sifted

FOR GANACHE:

3 cups whipping cream

12 ounces semisweet chocolate, melted

Preheat oven to 350° F. Butter and flour an 8-inch springform pan.

In bowl beat egg yolks until blended. In another bowl place egg whites and beat until soft peaks form. Sprinkle with sugar and mix in gently. Continue beating until stiff but not dry. Fold in egg yolks, cocoa, and flour.

Pour batter into prepared cake pan. Bake 20 to 25 minutes. Remove to rack to cool 5 minutes before frosting with ganache.

While cake is baking, make ganache. In top of double boiler over simmering water, warm 1 1/2 cups of the cream, 3 to 5 minutes. Remove from heat and stir in chocolate. Cool completely.

In bowl, whip remaining 1 1/2 cups cream until stiff peaks form. Gently fold into chocolate mixture.

Remove pan sides and slide cake onto serving plate. Frost top and sides with ganache.

TIRAMISÙ

SERVES 8

❋

THERE ARE MANY SUCCESSFUL HEARTLAND FOOD STORIES, BUT ONE OF MY FAVORITES IS THE STORY OF THE AURICCHIO CHEESE-MAKING FAMILY. THE AURICCHIOS HAVE BEEN PRODUCING CHEESE IN ITALY FOR FIVE GENERATIONS. IN THE LATE 1970S, THEY BEGAN MAKING CHEESE IN WISCONSIN. THEY NOW PRODUCE AWARD-WINNING PARMESAN, PROVOLONE, AND MASCARPONE CHEESE. THIS RECIPE IS FROM THE AURICCHIO FAMILY'S PRIVATE COLLECTION. SERVE WITH SWEETENED WHIPPED CREAM, IF DESIRED.

40 ladyfingers
Enough cold brewed espresso to soak ladyfingers
3 egg whites plus 6 egg yolks
1 cup sugar
1/4 cup Cognac
1 pound mascarpone
Powdered cocoa

In shallow dish place ladyfingers with enough cold espresso to soak them until they are moist but not disintegrating.

Select a 1 1/2-quart bowl. Using some of ladyfingers, make a single layer on bottom and along sides of bowl. Set aside.

Place egg whites in another bowl and beat until stiff peaks form. Set aside. In another bowl and using electric mixer, beat together egg yolks and sugar until light. Gradually adding Cognac and mascarpone continue beating until mixture is light and fluffy. Fold egg whites into cheese mixture.

Spoon one third of cheese mixture into ladyfinger-lined bowl. Cover with more ladyfingers. Continue until all of the cheese and ladyfingers have been used. Sprinkle cocoa over top. Cover lightly and refrigerate until ready to serve.

To serve spoon into shallow individual bowls.

CHOCOLATE-APPLE DACQUOISE

SERVES 8 TO 10

❋

CHEF LIZ CLARK'S UNUSUAL BLENDING OF APPLES AND CHOCOLATE IS AS BEAUTIFUL TO BEHOLD AS IT IS TASTY. LEAVE PLENTY OF TIME TO ASSEMBLE IT CAREFULLY. THEN SIT BACK AND WAIT FOR THE APPLAUSE.

Preheat oven to 300° F.

To prepare meringue, line baking sheet with parchment or buttered aluminum foil. In food processor fitted with steel blade, combine nuts and 1 cup sugar and process to a powder.

Place egg whites in a bowl and beat until frothy. Then, while gradually adding the remaining 3 tablespoons sugar, beat until stiff peaks form. Fold in vanilla and nut mixture.

Spoon meringue mixture into pastry bag fitted with plain tip. Pipe 3 rectangles,

FOR MERINGUE LAYERS:

1 cup pecans

1 cup plus 3 tablespoons sugar

1 cup egg whites (whites of 6 to 8 eggs)

1 teaspoon vanilla extract

FOR CHOCOLATE BUTTERCREAM:

5 ounces semisweet chocolate

1 ounce unsweetened chocolate

1/3 cup espresso or strong, brewed coffee, boiling

3 egg yolks

1/2 cup (1 stick) unsalted butter, cut into small pieces

1 teaspoon vanilla extract

1 tablespoon applejack or Calvados

FOR POACHED APPLE SLICES:

2 Granny Smith, Pippin, or Cortland apples, peeled, cored, and sliced

1 cup water

1/2 cup sugar

1/2 teaspoon vanilla extract

each about 5-by-9-inches, onto prepared baking sheet. Bake about 1 hour. Carefully peel meringues from parchment while still warm and set aside.

To prepare chocolate buttercream, place both chocolates in food processor fitted with steel blade. Process to a powder. With motor running, add boiling coffee in a steady stream. Then add the egg yolks and butter. Process until butter is thoroughly incorporated. Add vanilla and applejack and mix thoroughly.

FOR WHIPPED CREAM ICING:

2 cups whipping cream

3 tablespoons sugar

1 teaspoon vanilla extract

2 tablespoons applejack or Calvados

Fresh mint leaves and candied flowers, for garnish

To prepare apples, in saucepan combine apple slices, the water, sugar, and vanilla. Bring to boil. Reduce heat to low and simmer until apples are tender but not mushy. Drain, cool, and set aside.

To prepare icing, place cream in bowl and whip until stiff peaks form. Add sugar, vanilla, and applejack or Calvados. Set aside.

To assemble, place meringue layer on serving tray. Spread one third of chocolate buttercream on meringue. Top with half of apple slices. Place second meringue layer on top and repeat buttercream and apple layer. Place final meringue layer on top and ice with remaining buttercream. Chill.

Ice entire cake with whipped cream icing, reserving 1/2 cup. Spoon the 1/2 cup cream into pastry bag fitted with star tip and pipe rosettes in decorative pattern on top of the dacquoise. Garnish with mint leaves and candied flowers. Using a serrated knife slice carefully.

APPLE KRINGLE

SERVES 6

❋

RACINE, WISCONSIN, IS HOME OF THE APPLE KRINGLE. TRY ONE OF THESE YEASTED SWEET BREADS WARM FOR BRUNCH OR DESSERT.

Preheat oven to 375° F.

In small bowl dissolve yeast in the warm water and let stand until bubbly, 5 to 10 minutes.

Meanwhile, in small saucepan over medium heat, combine milk, butter, and sugar and scald. Cool to lukewarm.

Place flour in large bowl of electric mixer fitted with dough hook. Add yeast mixture, milk mixture, and egg and beat to make soft dough. Form into ball, place in bowl, and cover bowl lightly. Refrigerate for at least 2 hours or up to 24 hours.

1/2 package active dry yeast

1/4 cup warm (105° to 115° F) water

1/2 cup milk

5 tablespoons butter or margarine

4 tablespoons sugar

2 cups flour

1 egg

FOR APPLE FILLING:

2 cups Rome Beauty or other cooking apples

1/4 cup water

1/2 teaspoon ground cinnamon

1/2 teaspoon ground mace

1 tablespoon butter or margarine

FOR ICING:

1/4 cup confectioner's sugar

2 tablespoons milk

1/2 teaspoon vanilla extract

To make apple filling, in saucepan combine apples, the water, cinnamon, mace, and butter. Bring to boil, reduce heat to medium-low, and simmer, stirring occasionally, until tender, about 15 minutes. Transfer to blender or food processor fitted with steel blade and purée until smooth. Set aside.

Remove dough from refrigerator. On lightly floured board roll out dough into rectangle 15 inches long by 8 inches wide. Spread apple filling in center of rectangle. Fold long side over filling, overlapping filling by 1 inch. Seal edges by pressing lightly on dough. Using spatula, transfer to a lightly greased nonstick baking sheet.

Bake 20 minutes.

To make icing, sift sugar into bowl. Beat in milk and vanilla.

Remove kringle to serving dish. Drizzle with icing while warm. Best served warm. Cut crosswise into 2-inch strips.

CINNAMON-APPLE FRITTERS

SERVES 6

✹

APPLES SHOW UP OFTEN IN HEARTLAND RECIPES BECAUSE THEIR MANY VARIETIES GROW ABUN-
DANTLY THROUGHOUT THE MIDWEST. FOR DECADES EVERY FARM HAD ITS OWN APPLE
ORCHARD.

1 egg, lightly beaten

3 tablespoons sugar

1/4 teaspoon salt

1/4 teaspoon ground cinnamon

1 1/4 cups flour, sifted

1 teaspoon baking powder

1 cup milk

*3 large Red Delicious or other cooking apples, peeled, cored, cut
crosswise into slices 1/4 inch thick*

Canola oil, for frying

Confectioner's sugar

In shallow bowl stir together egg, sugar, salt, and cinnamon. Sift together flour and baking powder into small bowl. Whisk into egg mixture alternately with milk. Let batter stand 10 minutes. Stir.

Meanwhile, in deep sauté pan or saucepan pour in oil to depth of 1 inch and heat to 375° F. Working in batches of 4 slices, dip each apple slice into batter, coating well on both sides. Shake off excess batter and slide into oil. Fry until golden brown on first side, then turn and continue cooking until golden brown on second side, 30 to 45 seconds longer. Using slotted spoon remove to paper towels to drain briefly.

Sprinkle with confectioner's sugar and serve hot, allowing about 2 or 3 per serving.

RHUBARB CRISP

SERVES 6 TO 8

❋

CONSIDERED A FRUIT BY MOST COOKS AND DINERS, RHUBARB IS, IN FACT, A VEGETABLE. ITS LONG, CELERYLIKE STALKS ARE THE ONLY EDIBLE PART OF THE PLANT AND ARE EXTREMELY TART. THEY'RE OFTEN COMBINED WITH ANOTHER FRUIT—IN THIS CASE, DRIED CHERRIES.

3 1/2 cups cut-up, peeled rhubarb (1/2 in. pieces)

1/2 cup dried cherries

2/3 cup granulated sugar

1/3 cup cake flour

1/4 teaspoon each ground cinnamon and nutmeg

1 cup all-purpose flour

3/4 cup firmly packed light brown sugar

1/2 cup rolled oats

6 tablespoons (3/4 stick) butter, melted and cooled

Preheat oven to 375° F. Grease 9-inch round baking pan.

In bowl toss together rhubarb, cherries, granulated sugar, cake flour, cinnamon, and nutmeg. Arrange fruit in bottom of prepared pan.

In same bowl stir together all-purpose flour, brown sugar, oats, and butter. Sprinkle evenly over fruit. Pat down lightly with fingertips.

Bake until light golden brown, 30 to 35 minutes.

While still hot, cut into wedges and transfer to serving plate or individual dishes. Best served warm.

RHUBARB MOUSSE IN COOKIE TULIP

SERVES 4

❋

RHUBARB IS COMMONLY KNOWN AS PIE PLANT, A GOOD CLUE TO ITS MOST FREQUENT USE. HERE IT'S MADE INTO A LIGHT, TANGY MOUSSE AND SERVED ATTRACTIVELY IN A TULIP-SHAPED CRUST. HARLAN PETERSON CREATED THIS RECIPE IN HIS TAPAWINGO RESTAURANT IN ELLSWORTH, MICHIGAN (SEE PAGE 214).

FOR TULIPS:

6 tablespoons (3/4 stick) unsalted butter, at room temperature

1/4 cup sugar

1/2 cup unbleached flour, sifted

1/2 teaspoon vanilla extract

3 egg whites, at room temperature

Pinch salt

FOR MOUSSE:

1/2 pound rhubarb, peeled and finely diced

1/2 cup sugar

2 teaspoons unflavored gelatin

3 tablespoons cold water

1 cup whipping cream

Small fresh strawberries

Fresh mint leaves

Preheat oven to 425° F.

To make tulips, cut out four 7-inch rounds parchment paper. Butter rounds on one side. Place rounds on buttered baking sheets, buttered side up.

In bowl and using electric mixer, cream together butter and sugar until light and fluffy. Add flour and vanilla and stir just until combined.

In another bowl, combine the egg whites and salt. Beat until soft peaks form. Fold egg whites into the flour mixture, one fourth at a time. Spread 2 tablespoons batter in even layer on each buttered round, leaving 1/4-inch border around edge.

Bake until edges are golden, 4 to 6 minutes. Remove and invert each baked round, with parchment still attached, into small bowl. Peel off paper and pinch sides of each cookie to form tulip shape. Let cool 3 to 4 minutes, then transfer to rack to cool completely.

To make mousse, combine rhubarb and sugar in heavy saucepan over medium heat and bring to simmer. Simmer until rhubarb is soft, about 20 minutes. Set aside 1/4 cup of mixture. In food processor fitted with steel blade or in blender, purée remaining rhubarb mixture. Set aside.

In small saucepan sprinkle gelatin over the water and let soften 10 minutes. Then place over low heat until gelatin dissolves completely. Stir into rhubarb purée.

In bowl beat cream until stiff peaks form. Fold in rhubarb purée and cooked rhubarb. Cover and chill well.

Spoon chilled mousse into tulips and place on individual plates. Garnish with strawberries and mint leaves.

PLEASING PERSIMMON

The American persimmon, a small dense, full-flavored orange fruit, has been supplanted in many produce markets by the larger, milder Asian persimmon. However, in southern Indiana's town of Mitchell, the American variety reigns supreme as evidenced by the annual Persimmon Festival held the last week of September.

Persimmons, which grow wild, do not ripen after picking and are gathered from the ground after the ripe fruit has fallen. A much-sought-after delicacy, they are traditionally used in puddings and other desserts. On a small farm near Mitchell is possibly the only persimmon pulp canner in the world. Her name is Dymple Green, and she puts up about ten thousand cans of pulp each year. Working in a converted pony barn behind her house, Mrs. Green is aided by a machine invented by her husband, Vernon, that discards the seeds and skins.

Without the help of a machine, persimmons can be peeled by placing the stem side down, cutting a cross on the pointed end and peeling back the skin. They can then be sliced or cut in half to serve with other fruits or salads. Persimmons can also be frozen whole, then allowed to thaw slightly, for eating right out of the "shell."

PERSIMMON MOUSSE

SERVES 6

❋

USE FULLY RIPE PERSIMMONS, WHICH YIELD TO THE TOUCH WHEN GENTLY SQUEEZED.

12 small or 6 large persimmons

3/4 cup sugar

2 envelopes unflavored gelatin

1/2 cup water

1 teaspoon rum extract

1 cup whipping cream

1/4 cup rum

Using food processor fitted with steel blade or blender, purée persimmon pulp. You should have 3 cups purée. Set aside.

In small saucepan stir together 1/2 cup of the sugar and gelatin. Stir in water. Let stand 1 minute. Place over low heat and, stirring constantly, heat until gelatin dissolves, 2 to 3 minutes. Transfer to large bowl.

Add rum extract and 2 cups of the persimmon purée to gelatin mixture and mix well. Cover and refrigerate until mixture mounds slightly when dropped from spoon, about 1 hour.

Place cream in bowl and beat until stiff peaks form. Gently fold cream into gelatin mixture. Spoon into individual soufflé dishes or champagne flutes. Cover and refrigerate until firm, about 3 hours.

Meanwhile, in another bowl stir together remaining 1 cup persimmon purée, 1/4 cup sugar, and rum to form a sauce. Let stand 1 hour.

To serve, pour sauce over top.

VANILLA ICE CREAM SUNDAE

SERVES 4

❊

A MIDWEST LEGEND PLACES THE BIRTH OF THE ICE CREAM SUNDAE IN EVANSTON, ILLINOIS, IN THE EARLY 1880S. EVANSTON DRUGSTORE PROPRIETOR DECON GARWOOD DEVELOPED THE SUNDAE TO CIRCUMVENT A BLUE LAW THAT PROHIBITED SERVING SODA WATER ON SUNDAYS, THEREBY PROHIBITING ICE CREAM SODAS AS WELL. GARWOOD THOUGHT THE ICE CREAM SUNDAE A GOOD ALTERNATIVE AND AN IDEAL SUNDAY TREAT. HE WAS SO RIGHT!

FOR HOT FUDGE SAUCE:

2 cups (12 oz) semi-sweet chocolate chips

1 ounce dark chocolate

2 tablespoons corn syrup

1 tablespoon unsweetened cocoa powder

1 cup whipping cream

FOR SERVING:

Vanilla ice cream

Sweetened whipped cream

Chopped pecans

Maraschino cherries

To make the fudge sauce, place chocolates in double boiler over hot, not boiling, water. Stir occasionally. When fully melted stir in corn syrup and cocoa powder. Mix well. Add cream and heat until mixture is hot and sauce is smooth. Keep hot until serving.

When ready to serve sundaes, remove ice cream from freezer and place in refrigerator about 5 minutes to soften slightly.

To assemble sundaes, scoop ice cream into individual dessert dishes. Ladle hot fudge sauce over ice cream. Top with dollop of whipped cream, some pecans, and a cherry.

CHAPTER 11

Menus From Special Places in the Heartland

This chapter showcases memorable midwestern meals, just as they are served in some special places (and by some special people) in the Heartland. There's a heart-healthful Spa Luncheon menu from The Heartland, a health and fitness retreat and spa in Gilman, Illinois. There's Chef Harlan Peterson's traditional hearty Michigan Grill Dinner as served at Tapawingo, his lakeside restaurant in Ellsworth, Michigan. There's an Iowa  Fall Sunday Supper from the "first lady of Iowa cuisine," Chef Liz Clark. And there's a one-of-a-kind Midwest Christmas Dinner menu from Chef Carolyn Buster.

HEALTH AND THE HEARTLAND

An interest in healthy food and cooking techniques is nothing new to the Midwest. Almost a century ago, bran was touted as a cure-all for dyspepsia by Michigan's Dr. John Harvey Kellogg of cereal fame. Kellogg was influenced by the teachings of Sylvester Graham (the originator of the graham cracker), who saw salvation in bran as early as 1830.

In the mid-nineteenth century, water from a spring in Waukesha, Wisconsin, was purported to have curative qualities. As the water's fame spread, townspeople built hotels and resorts for travelers who came to "take the waters" at the source. Eventually Waukesha water was bottled under the well-known White Rock Water label.

Over the years nutrition has become big business throughout the Midwest. Illinois, for example, is home to the NutraSweet Company; Canfield's, bottlers of a highly popular chocolate diet soda; and Hess and Hunt, pioneering nutritional consultants based in the Chicago area.

Today in the Heartland the number one rule for healthy dining is recognizing that there are no "bad" foods. The emphasis is on enjoying reasonably sized portions—appreciating the taste of good food without overindulgence. Equally important is learning to make nutrition-wise choices. For example, in many recipes canola oil (a Midwest product!) can replace less healthful saturated fats. Low-fat foods can help balance the total intake of dietary fat in daily menus. And while the Heartland Food Society Cookbook was never intended to be a collection of diet recipes, the nutritional profile of many of the recipes in this book can easily be modified to meet individual needs.

HEARTLAND SPA LUNCHEON

SERVES 8

BLACK BEAN BURRITOS

CONFETTI RELISH

GUACAMOLE SAUCE

MOCK SOUR CREAM

SPANISH RICE

The Heartland, a health-and-fitness retreat center and spa in Gilman, Illinois, has all the fine appointments of a complete spa with the added attraction of midwestern charm and friendliness. Situated in a gracious, sprawling former gentleman's farm about eighty miles south of Chicago, it offers fitness training; relaxation; diet and nutritional counseling; and exercise, spa, and sports facilities. This luncheon menu from the Heartland demonstrates how tasty and healthy spa fare can be.

HEARTLAND SPA LUNCHEON

BLACK BEAN BURRITOS

❋

ANY LEFTOVER COOKED WHOLE BLACK BEANS OR BLACK BEAN PURÉE CAN BE FROZEN FOR FUTURE USE.

Preheat oven to 400° F.

To make bean purée, combine all ingredients in food processor fitted with steel blade. Purée until fairly smooth.

To assemble burritos, spread about 2 tablespoons of the bean purée down the middle of each tortilla. Top each with 1/4 cup lettuce, 1 ounce diced tomato, 1/2 ounce cheese, and 1 tablespoon green onion. Roll up each tortilla, folding in ends. Arrange seam sides down on baking sheet.

Bake until heated through, about 10 minutes. Serve on individual plates. Top each burrito with Guacamole Sauce and Mock Sour Cream. Scatter few whole cooked beans over each plate.

Note: One pound dried black beans will yield about 6 cups cooked beans.

FOR BLACK BEAN PURÉE:

1 1/2 cups cooked black beans (see note)

1 tablespoon salad seasoning such as Mrs. Dash brand

1/2 teaspoon chili powder

1/4 teaspoon dried cilantro

1/4 cup water

8 chapatis or whole-wheat tortillas

2 1/4 cups finely shredded lettuce

8 ounces finely diced tomato

4 ounces finely shredded low-fat Colby or Cheddar cheese

8 tablespoons finely sliced green onion

Guacamole Sauce (see page 212)

Mock Sour Cream (see page 212)

Whole cooked black beans, for garnish

HEARTLAND SPA LUNCHEON
CONFETTI RELISH

❋

THIS COLORFUL RELISH TASTES BEST WHEN PREPARED A DAY IN ADVANCE OF SERVING. IT WILL KEEP WELL IN THE REFRIGERATOR FOR UP TO ONE WEEK.

1/2 cup cider vinegar

2 tablespoons fructose

1 tablespoon chopped fresh cilantro

1 clove garlic, minced or pressed

1 1/2 ounces red onion, diced

6 ounces sweet pepper (red and/or yellow), diced

6 ounces cucumber, seeded and diced

6 ounces jicama, peeled and diced

3 ounces cooked black beans

In nonreactive saucepan combine vinegar, fructose, cilantro, and garlic and bring to boil. Remove from heat and pour into stainless-steel or glass bowl. Stir in onion and allow to cool to room temperature.

Stir in bell pepper, cucumber, jicama, and beans. Cover and refrigerate until thoroughly chilled.

HEARTLAND SPA LUNCHEON

GUACAMOLE SAUCE

❉

In food processor fitted with steel blade, combine all ingredients. Purée until smooth. Chill thoroughly before serving.

Note: To make a thicker guacamole for dipping, do not process the tomato with remaining ingredients. Instead, substitute 3 seeded and diced tomatoes (about 2 cups) and stir into the processed mixture. Chill.

15 ounces low-fat ricotta cheese

1 avocado, peeled and pitted

1 tomato, seeded (see Note)

3 green onions, coarsely chopped

1 clove garlic

1/2 cup plain nonfat yogurt

1 tablespoon fresh lemon juice

1/2 teaspoon each ground cumin and ground coriander

2 teaspoons Dijon-style mustard

2 teaspoons salad seasoning such as Mrs. Dash brand

Hot sauce, to taste

HEARTLAND SPA LUNCHEON

MOCK SOUR CREAM

❉

THIS LOW-FAT TOPPING CAN BE SUBSTITUTED FOR SOUR CREAM IN BOTH MAIN DISHES AND DESSERTS.

4 cups plain nonfat yogurt

In bowl place a cheesecloth-lined colander. Spoon yogurt into colander. Cover, refrigerate, and let drain at least 4 hours or overnight. Discard the water (whey) that accumulates.

HEARTLAND SPA LUNCHEON

SPANISH RICE

❋

SERVE ALONGSIDE BLACK BEAN BURRITO (SEE PAGE 210).

2 cups vegetable stock

1 cup brown rice

1 teaspoon olive oil

3 tablespoons (1 oz) diced green sweet pepper

3 tablespoons (1 oz) diced onion

1 teaspoon ground cumin

1/2 teaspoon dried oregano

1/2 teaspoon dried basil

1/2 cup crushed tomatoes

In saucepan bring stock to boil. Add rice, stir once, and cover tightly. Reduce heat to low and cook until tender, about 45 minutes.

In skillet over medium heat, warm oil. Add pepper and onion and sauté until tender, about 5 minutes. Add cumin, oregano, and basil. Sauté 30 seconds longer. Add tomatoes and rice and stir to combine well and heat through.

Serve immediately.

MICHIGAN GRILL DINNER
CHEF HARLAN PETERSON

CREAM OF SPRING GREENS SOUP

MIXED GRILL WITH FRESH THYME AND MAPLE-GLAZED ONIONS

RUSTIC APPLE PIE

SERVES 8

In 1984, Harlan Peterson bought a seven-acre lakeside residence in Ellsworth, Michigan. The historic resort on the property was converted into a restaurant and given the Chippewa name Tapawingo, meaning "restful place" or "place of joy." This grill menu from Chef Peterson's restaurant emphasizes the choicest of local ingredients presented with elegant simplicity.

MICHIGAN GRILL DINNER

CREAM OF SPRING GREENS SOUP

❋

IF YOU PREFER TO SERVE THIS SOUP HOT, REHEAT THE PURÉED SOUP BASE WITH THE CREAM AND THEN ADD THE SEASONINGS. OMIT THE CHERVIL GARNISH.

4 cups rich chicken stock

4 potatoes, unpeeled, roughly chopped

1 pound asparagus, stalks cut into 1-inch pieces and tips reserved

2 cups stemmed tender spinach leaves

2 cups stemmed tender sorrel leaves

2 cups stemmed watercress leaves

2 cups whipping cream, chilled

Salt, freshly ground pepper, and freshly grated nutmeg, to taste

Fresh chervil sprigs for garnish

In heavy stainless-steel saucepan, combine stock and potatoes and bring to boil. Reduce heat and cook about 5 minutes. Add asparagus stalks and cook until potatoes and asparagus are just tender. Add spinach, sorrel, and watercress and stir well. Immediately remove from heat and cool.

Working in batches, purée potato mixture. Strain through fine sieve into bowl, cover, and chill.

Meanwhile, blanch reserved asparagus tips in boiling salted water 1 minute. Drain and shock under cold running water. Drain again and reserve.

When soup base is chilled, stir in cream, salt, pepper, and nutmeg. (Add more chicken stock and/or cream if thinner soup is desired.)

Ladle soup into shallow soup bowls and garnish with asparagus tips and chervil sprigs. Serve at once.

MICHIGAN GRILL DINNER

MIXED GRILL WITH FRESH THYME AND MAPLE-GLAZED ONIONS

AN UPSCALE HEARTLAND VERSION OF THE TRADITIONAL MIXED GRILL.

Coat lamb and veal with oil, then season with thyme, salt, and pepper. Cover with waxed paper and let stand 2 hours at room temperature.

While meat marinates, begin to prepare onions. Preheat oven to 400° F. Fill saucepan three-fourths full with water and bring to boil. Add onions and cook briskly about 1 minute. Drain. Using small sharp knife, trim off stem ends, slip off

FOR GRILL:

8 prime lamb chops, each cut from 2 ribs and then 1 rib removed

8 prime veal medallions (3 oz each) cut from loin

Olive oil, as needed

2 tablespoons chopped fresh thyme

Salt and freshly ground pepper, to taste

FOR GLAZED ONIONS:

24 small boiling onions, unpeeled (about 1 in. in diameter)

1/2 cup butter

6 tablespoons maple syrup

1 teaspoon salt

8 links spicy duck sausage

1 cup Heartland Cabernet Sauvignon or other dry red wine

3 cups clarified rich veal stock

24 fresh thyme sprigs

white, parchmentlike skins, and cut off tops. Arrange onions in baking dish just large enough to hold them in single layer.

In small skillet over medium heat melt butter. When foam subsides, add maple syrup and salt and stir until mixture is hot. Pour over onions, turning them with spoon to coat evenly. Bake onions in oven, basting occasionally with cooking liquid, until golden brown and there is no resistance when pierced deeply with point of small knife, about 40 minutes.

Meanwhile, preheat grill.

About 20 minutes before onions are ready, in sauté pan over high heat, pour in enough oil to form thin film. Heat until just smoking. Add lamb chops and veal and sear briefly on both sides. Transfer to preheated grill and set sauté pan aside unwashed. Place duck sausage on grill. Grill veal about 4 minutes per side, lamb about 5 minutes per side, and sausage about 8 minutes total cooking time, turning several times. Remove all meats from heat, cover to keep warm, and let rest 5 minutes.

Pour off excess fat from sauté pan used for lamb chops and veal. Place over high heat, add red wine, and deglaze, stirring to dislodge browned bits. Reduce wine until nearly evaporated. Add stock and reduce to about 1 cup. Season with salt and pepper.

Arrange 1 lamb chop, 1 veal medallion, and 1 portion duck sausage on one third of each warmed dinner plate. Strain sauce through fine sieve and pour enough on each plate to cover plate thinly. Spoon 3 glazed onions in center of plate and garnish with thyme sprigs, one between each portion of meat. Serve immediately.

MICHIGAN GRILL DINNER

RUSTIC APPLE PIE

A MIDWEST VARIATION ON AN ALL-AMERICAN CLASSIC—THE PERFECT ENDING TO A MIXED GRILL DINNER.

FOR PASTRY:

3 cups flour

1 1/2 cups confectioner's sugar

1 cup (2 sticks) unsalted butter, cut into 1/2-inch pieces

2 egg yolks

1 teaspoon grated lemon zest

1/2 teaspoon vanilla extract

Ice water, if needed

FOR FILLING:

8 apples, peeled, cored, and sliced

3/4 cup sugar

2 teaspoons ground cinnamon

Juice of 1/2 lemon

1/4 cup butter, cut into bits

1 egg, beaten with 1/4 cup water

To make pastry, in bowl stir together flour and sugar. Add butter, egg yolks, lemon zest, and vanilla. Mix just until dough starts to form. If necessary, add several drops of ice water to help bind. Gather into ball, wrap, and refrigerate 1 hour.

Preheat oven to 350° F.

On lightly floured board roll out dough into 14-inch round. Transfer to large baking sheet.

To make filling, in bowl toss together apple slices, sugar, cinnamon, and lemon juice.

Mound apples on pastry, leaving 3-inch border on all sides. Dot with butter.

Brush edges of pastry with some of egg-water mixture. Working in small sections, fold pastry border over apples; brush overlaps with more egg-water mixture and press together gently. Leave apple center exposed.

Bake until pastry is golden brown and apples are tender, about 1 hour. Serve warm.

IOWA FALL SUNDAY SUPPER

CHEF LIZ CLARK

AUTUMN VEGETABLE SOUP WITH HAZELNUT PESTO

WILD DUCK AND QUAIL PÂTÉ

UPTOWN CHICKEN POT PIE

PUMPKIN CRÈME CARAMEL

SERVES 6

After nearly two decades of experience, Elizabeth Clark, a charter member of the Heartland Food Society, has truly become Iowa's first lady of cuisine. From a farm upbringing to a worldwide education in ethnic and contemporary culinary techniques, Clark has combined her talents and vibrant imagination in creative ways that have helped put her home state on the culinary map.

Liz Clark's Cooking School and Restaurant are located on the bluffs above the Mississippi in Keokuk, Iowa. She offers an extremely popular calendar of culinary classes, including Stews and Breads for a Mid-Winter Evening, How to Cook His Goose and Other Wild Game, and Breads, Grills and Grains from the Mediterranean Basin. Clark also prepares and serves single-party, by-reservation-only gourmet dinners at a huge mahogany dining table in her gracious nineteenth-century Italian Revival mansion, which recently has been placed on the National Register of Historic Places.

Whether preparing meals from her personally designed menus or creating a custom feast to satisfy special requests, Liz Clark takes advantage of the seasonal bounty offered by local gardens, as evidenced by her fall Sunday supper menu.

IOWA FALL SUNDAY SUPPER

AUTUMN VEGETABLE SOUP
WITH HAZELNUT PESTO

❀

ENCOURAGE YOUR GUESTS TO STIR THE FRAGRANT PESTO TOPPING INTO THE SOUP JUST BEFORE EATING.

To make pesto, cut cheese into 1/2-inch chunks. In food processor fitted with steel blade, grind cheese by dropping in a few pieces at a time through the feed tube. Add garlic cloves and hazelnuts and continue to process until cheese pieces are finely ground. Add parsley and pulse until thoroughly combined. With the motor running, add enough olive oil through the feed tube for mixture to form a paste. Season to taste with pepper.

To make soup, in large enameled cast-iron dutch oven, over medium heat pour

FOR PESTO:

3 ounces Parmesan cheese, about 1 cup

5 cloves garlic

3/4 cup hazelnuts

1 bunch fresh flat-leaf parsley

1/2 to 3/4 cup extra virgin olive oil

Freshly ground pepper

FOR SOUP:

Extra virgin olive oil, as needed

3 onions, finely chopped

4 cloves garlic, minced

3 bay leaves

2 teaspoons thyme

3 quarts chicken stock

*2 1/4 cups (1/2 lb) Great Northern beans, soaked overnight
   in water to cover*

4 carrots, peeled and diced

1 red bell pepper, seeded and chopped

3 green bell peppers, seeded and chopped

2 large tomatoes, peeled, seeded, and chopped

in enough olive oil to cover pan bottom. Add onions, garlic, bay leaves, and thyme and sauté, stirring constantly, until onions are translucent, about 5 minutes. Pour in chicken stock. Add beans, along with their soaking liquid, and carrots. Bring to boil and reduce heat to low. Simmer until beans are soft.

4 turnips, peeled and diced

1 small winter squash (such as buttercup), peeled, seeded, and diced

2 yellow zucchini, diced

2 small green zucchini, diced

1/4 pound fresh mushrooms, sliced

1/4 head green cabbage, shredded

Stir in bell peppers, tomatoes, turnips, and winter squash and continue to simmer until squash is tender. Add yellow and green zucchini and mushrooms and simmer a few minutes longer. Stir in cabbage and cook just until cabbage wilts.

Discard bay leaves. Ladle soup into bowls and top each with a heaping spoonful of pesto.

IOWA FALL SUNDAY SUPPER
WILD DUCK AND QUAIL PÂTÉ

❋

SERVE WITH MUSTARD, CORNI-
CHONS (PICKLED GHERKINS),
AND CRUSTY BREAD.

2 mallards, canvasbacks, or other wild ducks, cleaned

6 quail, cleaned

1 whole chicken breast

1 pound bacon, sliced

1 onion, coarsely chopped

1 extra-large egg

2 teaspoons dried thyme

Freshly grated nutmeg

2 teaspoons sea salt

1 teaspoon freshly ground white pepper

3 bay leaves

Bone out both duck breasts and skin halves; set breast halves aside. Remove remaining meat from carcasses, discard skin, and place meat in a food processor fitted with steel blade. Skin and bone quail and chicken breast.

Coarsely chop both meats along with slices of the bacon. Add these meats to processor with onion, egg, thyme, a good grating of nutmeg, sea salt, and white pepper. Process until mixture is finely ground and well combined.

Wrap each of the 4 reserved duck breast halves in a slice of bacon. Line a covered ceramic pâté dish or loaf pan with the remaining bacon slices, allowing them to overhang the sides.

Preheat oven to 350° F.

Make layer of one third of ground meat mixture in lined dish. Place 2 wrapped breast halves end to end on top and press down firmly to embed them. Add half of remaining ground meat mixture and embed remaining 2 breast halves. Top with remaining ground meat mixture, smoothing to cover breasts completely. Tap dish firmly on countertop to settle pâté and remove any air pockets. Bring up overhanging bacon slices to cover top of pâté. Place bay leaves in line on top. Cover dish with lid or, if using loaf pan, cover tightly with aluminum foil.

Put pâté dish in deep roasting pan and place on center rack of oven. Pour boiling water into roasting pan to come halfway up sides of pâté dish. Bake 1 1/2 hours.

Remove from oven and let cool completely. Place weight on pâté and refrigerate several hours or overnight. (A foil-wrapped brick works well as a weight.)

Unmold and slice carefully to reveal mosaic pattern of whole duck and chicken breasts in forcemeat.

‖

IOWA FALL SUNDAY SUPPER
UPTOWN CHICKEN POT PIE

❈

THE PUFF PASTRY DOUGH CAN BE MADE AHEAD AND FROZEN FOR USE WHEN NEEDED.

FOR PUFF PASTRY:

1 cup plus 1 tablespoon unbleached flour

1 cup plus 1 tablespoon unbleached pastry flour

1 teaspoon salt

1 cup (2 sticks) lightly salted chilled butter

1/2 to 3/4 cup water, chilled

To make pastry, in food processor fitted with steel blade, combine flours and salt. Cut 1/2 cup of the butter into small pieces. Add to processor. Process until mixture resembles cornmeal. With motor running add enough of the cold water through feed tube until mixture forms ball and cleans sides of bowl.

Turn dough out onto floured pastry cloth and roll out into rough rectangle about 12 inches by 16 inches. Cut remaining 1/2 cup butter into thirds and refrigerate two thirds of it. Cut remaining third into pea-sized pieces and distribute over surface of dough. Work quickly to avoid having the warmth of your hands melt butter.

Using pastry cloth to help manipulate dough, fold dough into thirds like a business letter, enclosing butter. From narrow end, fold in thirds again to make compact package. Put pastry in plastic bag and refrigerate at least 15 minutes. (Do not place in freezer to accelerate chilling.) After chilling, reflour cloth and roll out pastry again. (This time dough rectangle will be more even.) Roll at right angles to rectangle; do not roll diagonally or butter will not be evenly distributed and break through corners of dough. Again, cut half of remaining chilled butter into pea-shaped pieces and distribute over the dough. Fold as before and chill another 15 minutes.

After second chilling repeat the rolling-out process one more time with remaining butter. Chill again 15 minutes and pastry is ready to use. (At this point the pastry can be frozen.)

To make filling, in enameled cast-iron dutch oven over medium-high heat, melt 1/4 cup of the butter. Add thyme, bay leaves, chicken, and onion and sauté until onion is translucent and chicken is opaque but not browned.

Stir in carrots and celery, reduce heat, and continue to stir constantly. Add mushrooms and bouillon cube, stirring to dissolve cube. Simmer until vegetables are crisp-tender. Add asparagus

FOR FILLING:

1/2 cup (1 stick) butter, divided

1 teaspoon dried thyme

3 bay leaves

2 whole chicken breasts, boned, skinned, and diced

1 large onion, diced

3 carrots, peeled and cut into 3-inch-long strips about 1/4-inch square

3 celery stalks, cut into 3-inch-long strips

1/2 ounce dried mushrooms (such as cèpes or morels), soaked for about 30 minutes in 1/2 cup warm water, drained, and liquid reserved

1 chicken bouillon cube (Knorr or Maggi brand preferred)

6 asparagus, cut into 2-inch lengths

3 tablespoons flour

1/2 cup dry white wine or sherry

Salt and freshly ground pepper

1 egg, beaten with 1 tablespoon cold water

and cook 2 minutes longer. Pour chicken-vegetable mixture through sieve, capturing liquid in bowl. Set chicken-vegetable mixture and liquid aside separately.

In sauté pan over medium heat, melt remaining butter. Add flour and cook, stirring constantly, about 4 minutes. Stir in reserved liquid, wine or sherry, and simmer, stirring, until thickened. Add chicken-vegetable mixture. Taste and adjust seasoning with salt and pepper, if needed. Cover and keep warm.

Preheat oven to 375° F.

Select 6 small casserole or onion soup dishes. On floured pastry cloth, roll out pastry about 1/4-inch thick. Using bottom of individual casserole or onion soup dish as guide, cut out 6 rounds. Transfer rounds to ungreased baking sheet and prick in few places with fork. If desired, cut out leaves and roses from pastry scraps, brush with egg-water mixture, and place on dough rounds. Then brush rounds and decorations with remaining egg-water mixture.

Bake until puffed and golden, about 15 minutes.

Meanwhile, warm serving dishes. Divide the warm chicken and vegetables evenly among them. Top each with a puff-pastry lid and serve immediately.

IOWA FALL SUNDAY SUPPER

PUMPKIN CRÈME CARAMEL

✳

Preheat oven to 350° F. Bake pumpkins on a baking sheet until soft, about 30 minutes. Cool.

Cut pumpkins in half and discard seeds. Peel and cut flesh into chunks. In food processor purée pumpkin chunks until smooth. You should have about 1 cup.

2 small Jack-o-Lite pumpkins

3/4 cup plus 3 tablespoons sugar

1/4 cup water

2 cups milk

2 whole eggs plus 3 egg yolks

1/2 teaspoon each ground cinnamon and ginger

Freshly grated nutmeg, to taste

1 teaspoon vanilla extract

2 tablespoons dark rum (Meyers preferred)

Boiling water, as needed

In heavy saucepan over medium-high heat, bring and 3/4 cup sugar and water to boil. Watch constantly; sugar will begin to caramelize. When mixture is golden brown, remove from heat and pour into a 1 1/2-quart soufflé dish. Tilt quickly to coat dish bottom evenly with caramel. Cool.

Pour milk into saucepan and scald; cool slightly. In bowl whisk together whole eggs and yolks, 3 tablespoons sugar, cinnamon, ginger, nutmeg, vanilla, and rum. Slowly pour warm milk through sieve into egg mixture, whisking constantly. Add pumpkin purée and whisk in thoroughly. Pour egg mixture into prepared soufflé dish. Place dish in roasting pan and pour in boiling water to come halfway up sides of dish.

Bake until knife inserted in center comes out clean, about 45 minutes. Cool completely.

To serve, run knife around edge of custard to loosen from dish sides. Invert serving platter over soufflé dish and, holding dish and platter together firmly, lift off soufflé dish.

MIDWEST CHRISTMAS DINNER
CHEF CAROLYN BUSTER

SMOKED FISH PÂTÉ

WILD MUSHROOM, CHESTNUT, AND PUMPKIN BISQUE

PARTRIDGE IN A PEAR TREE

RASPBERRY CAKE

SERVES 6

Carolyn Buster began her cooking career by apprenticing herself to several fine Chicago chefs. For the past twenty years, she has been the chef/owner of an exclusive, prize-winning restaurant in Calumet City, Illinois. An honorary doctorate degree in culinary arts from Johnson and Wales University, Providence, Rhode Island, was awarded to her in 1991.

Chef Buster created this exquisite Christmas feast especially for this book.

MIDWEST CHRISTMAS DINNER

Smoked Fish Pâté

❋

SERVE THIS DELICATE PÂTÉ
WITH TOAST POINTS.

In food processor fitted with
steel blade, combine apple,
horseradish, and lemon juice.
Process until texture of apple
is medium-fine. Remove to
bowl and mix in green
onions.

Place fish, pepper, garlic,
and salt in food processor and
process until well blended. Alternatively, run twice through a food grinder. If fish is
extremely dry, during processing or grinding add room-temperature butter, sour cream,
or mayonnaise as needed to moisten.

Remove fish mixture to serving bowl and fold in apple mixture and orange zest. Serve
at room temperature.

1 small tart apple, cored and cut up

1 1/2 tablespoons horseradish

1 teaspoon fresh lemon juice

3 green onions, minced

1 pound smoked fish (such as trout), skinned and boned

1/2 teaspoon freshly ground white pepper

Pinch garlic powder

1/2 teaspoon salt

*Butter (at room temperature), sour cream, or mayonnaise, as
     needed*

Zest of 1 orange

MIDWEST CHRISTMAS DINNER

WILD MUSHROOM, CHESTNUT, AND PUMPKIN BISQUE

❋

USING A COMBINATION OF FRESH AND DRIED MUSHROOMS INTENSIFIES THE FLAVOR OF THIS CREAM SOUP.

In heavy saucepan over medium heat, melt butter. Add pumpkin, celery, onion, carrot, garlic, parsley, bay leaves, allspice, and pepper. Sauté, stirring occasionally, until vegetables are soft; do not brown.

Add fresh and reconstituted mushrooms along with soaking liquid and veal and chicken stocks. Simmer about 30 minutes. Stir in chestnut purée and cook 10 to 15 minutes longer, or until vegetables are very soft

1 cup (2 sticks) butter

4 cups diced, peeled pumpkin or butternut squash

3 cups diced celery

1 cup each diced onion and carrot

4 or 5 cloves garlic, pressed

3 to 4 tablespoons chopped fresh parsley

3 or 4 bay leaves

1/2 teaspoon each ground allspice and white pepper

1 pound fresh button mushrooms, chopped

1/4 pound dried cèpes (porcini), soaked 30 minutes in 2 cups warm water

6 cups veal stock

4 cups chicken stock

1 can (32 oz) chestnut purée

6 cups whipping cream

1/2 cup Cognac

1 cup dry sherry

Salt, to taste

Whipped cream flavored with Cognac, for garnish

Freshly roasted chestnuts, peeled and chopped, for garnish

and purée is incorporated.

Cool slightly. Working in batches, purée in blender and then strain through fine sieve onto clean plate. Stir in cream, Cognac, and dry sherry. Taste and adjust seasoning with salt, if necessary.

Reheat gently. Garnish with Cognac-flavored whipped cream and chopped chestnuts before serving.

MIDWEST WINE COUNTRY

Areas renowned for fine wine: France. California. Italy. Germany. Wisconsin. Wisconsin?

Yes, Wisconsin. Also Michigan, Illinois, Indiana, and other midwestern states. In the nineteenth century the founders of wineries in these states showed the then-newborn California wine industry that a wine need not be imported to be graceful.

It was the work of Agostin Haraszthy, a Hungarian expatriate and father of the California wine industry, that connected the two regions. Working first in vineyard bluffs around Prairie du Sac, Wisconsin, and later in Sonoma County, California, he established vineyards in both areas that are still producing.

Most of the wines of the Prairie du Sac area in Wisconsin are from French-American hybrid grape varieties: Marechal Foch, Millot, Seyval Blanc. Illinois and Indiana favor traditional French varieties: Merlot, Chardonnay, Cabernet Sauvignon, Pinot Noir. Fruit wines—blackberry, pear, and rhubarb, among others—also are a specialty of the Midwest, particularly Illinois. Michigan, thanks to areas with favorable micro climates, produces a number of excellent table wines made from Riesling and other German varieties, as well as notable French wines, including Chardonnay, and some distinguished sherries.

Although the Midwest may not be the first area to come to mind when connoisseurs contemplate fine wines, wine making is nevertheless thriving in the land that gave other wine making regions their start.

MIDWEST CHRISTMAS DINNER

PARTRIDGE IN A PEAR TREE

❋

THE "PEAR TREES" (MADE OF CHESTNUT AND SPINACH PURÉES) FOR THIS DISH CAN BE PIPED
ONTO THE SERVING PLATES IN ADVANCE OF SERVING. PARTRIDGE IS AVAILABLE AT GOURMET
FOOD STORES AND THROUGH MAIL-ORDER RESOURCES (SEE PAGES 236—237).

6 partridge breasts

Apple cider, to cover partridges

Wood chips, soaked 30 minutes in water to cover and drained

Clarified butter, as needed for sautéing

1 cup canned chestnut purée, seasoned with salt and white
pepper

1 cup fresh spinach purée, stabilized with 2 egg yolks

Finely julienned leeks, deep-fried until crisp

6 small poached pears

Place partridge breasts in nonreactive container and add apple cider to cover. Cover and marinate at least 24 hours.

Drain breasts and pat dry. In skillet over medium heat melt clarified butter. Sauté breasts turning once, until just tender, about 5 minutes total cooking time. Do not overcook. Keep warm.

Warm 6 large dinner plates. Using the chestnut purée, form a pear tree trunk on each plate. Use fork tines to give finished barklike appearance. Spoon spinach purée into pastry bag and pipe an outline to form branches of pear tree. (Plates can be prepared ahead of time up to this point, carefully covered with plastic wrap, and held at room temperature until time to serve.)

On each plate place a partridge breast, along with a pear, inside spinach purée outline. Drizzle remaining clarified butter over breast and pear. Decorate base of tree trunk with fried leeks, to resemble grass. Serve immediately.

⫶

MIDWEST CHRISTMAS DINNER

RASPBERRY CAKE

❋

FRESH RASPBERRIES SERVED ON THE SIDE ARE AN ELEGANT ADDITION TO THIS UNUSUAL CHRISTMAS CAKE.

1 1/2 pounds 1- or 2-day-old French or Vienna bread, crusts discarded and cut into 1/2-inch-thick slices

2 cups (4 sticks) butter, at room temperature

2 cups sugar

6 to 8 cups fresh-frozen raspberries, defrosted (with liquid reserved)

4 cups sour cream or crème frâiche, flavored with 2 tablespoons light brown sugar, or more, to taste

Butter inside of 9-inch springform pan, with 3-inch deep sides. Dust with sugar. Butter one side of each bread slice. Completely line bottom and sides of pan with some of the bread slices, pressing buttered sides against pan.

Generously spread additional butter over bread-lined mold. Sprinkle with approximately 1/2 cup of the sugar, add half of the raspberries along with juice and then sprinkle with another 1/2 cup sugar. Add another layer of buttered bread, buttered side up, then sprinkle with 1/2 cup more sugar. Top with remaining raspberries and juice. Finish with another layer of buttered bread and top with remaining 1/2 cup sugar. Place a flat plate on top, weight down evenly, and chill 6 hours or more.

To serve, unmold by quickly dipping base of mold in hot water. Immediately invert mold onto platter. Lift off mold. Serve with sweetened sour cream.

⫶

MAIL-ORDER SOURCES

Jaarsma Bakery
727 Franklin
Pella, IA 50219
(515) 628-2940
Marzipan cookies

Lewright Meats
Paul Bubeck
108 North Iowa Street
Eagle Grove, IA 50533
(515) 448-4286
Smoked pork loin, chops, sausages, cured ham, bacon

Maytag Cheese Company
Box 806
Newton, IA 50208
(515) 792-1133
Blue cheese

Michigan Marketing Association
1118 North Walnut Street
Lansing, MI 48006
(517) 371-2411
Wild mushrooms, edible flowers, fiddlehead ferns, baby white asparagus

Nauvoo Mill and Bakery
1530 Mulholland Street
Nauvoo, IL 62354
(217) 453-6734
Blue cheese, whole-wheat flour

Peoples Smoke and Grill
Cumberland, Rhode Island
(800) 729-5800
Gourmet cooking woods: hickory, apple, cherry, maple, maple/cob, peach, and more

Plath's Meats, Inc.
P.O. Box 7
Rogers City, MI 49779
(517) 734-2232
Smoked pork loin, chops, sugar-cured hams and bacon, turkey breast, chicken, whitefish

Tree Mendous Fruit Orchards
Eau Clair, MI 49111
(616) 782-7101
Boutique apples

Wauconda Orchards
1201 Gossell Road
Wauconda, IL 60084
(708) 526-8553
Apples

Whistling Wings
113 Washington Street
Hanover, IL 61041
(815) 591-2206
Mallard ducks

Wild Game, Inc.
2315 West Huron Street
Chicago, IL 60622
(312) 287-1661
*Shiitake mushrooms, farm-raised game, free-
range chickens and turkeys, partridges,
poussin, venison, buffalo*

INDEX

CREDITS

Auricchio family, Green Bay, Wisconsin: Tiramisù, 195

Jean Banchet, Wheeling, Illinois: Jean Banchet Chocolate Cake, 194

Mr. and Mrs. John Boder, Boder's-on-the-River, Mequon, Wisconsin: Seven Greens Soup, 59

Russell Bry, Executive Chef, Lettuce Entertain You Enterprises, Inc., Chicago, Illinois: Roasted Vegetable and Chicken Hash, 26

Carolyn Buster, Calumet City, Illinois: Midwest Christmas Dinner, 228–234

Linda Califore, CHIC, Cooking and Hospitality Institute of Chicago, (Illinois): Chutney Pork Roast, 20

Chicago Architecture Foundation, Chicago, Illinois: Glessner Diary excerpt, "Chicago's Elite," 36

Milos Cihelka, Golden Mushroom Restaurant, Southfield, Michigan: Wild Mushroom Strudel, 46

Liz Clark, Liz Clark's Restaurant and Cooking School, Keokuk, Iowa: Iowa Fall Sunday Supper, 219–227

Rita Dodd, Dodd's Townhouse, Indianapolis, Indiana: Dodd's Buttermilk Pie, 185

Peter J. George, Peter's Restaurant, Indianapolis, Indiana: Game Sausage with Smoked Apples, Grilled Onions, and Maple Cream Sauce, 50

The Heartland, Gilman, Illinois: Heartland Spa Luncheon, 209–213

Michael Higgins, Maldaner's Restaurant, Springfield, Illinois: Smoked Trout Cheesecake with Sweet-and-Sour Red Onions, 38

Kay Owen's Restaurant and LaCorsett's Maison Inn, Newton, Iowa: Medallions of Pork with Mushrooms, 140

Charlene Korslund, Eagle Grove, Iowa: Norwegian Potato Cakes, 162

Thierry Le Feuvre, Froggy's French Cafe, Highwood, Illinois: Terrine of Chicken and Wild Mushrooms, 114

Marshall Field's, Chicago, Illinois: Frango® Chocolate Brownies, 33

Arnold Morton, Arnie's Restaurant, Chicago, Illinois: Vegetable Soufflé with Sweet Red Pepper Sauce, 154

Marian Whalen Murphy, Whistling Wings, Hanover, Illinois: Mallard with Cranberries, 128

The Nashville House, Inc., Nashville, Indiana: Fried Biscuits with Apple Butter, 80

Harlan W. Peterson, Tapawingo Restaurant, Ellsworth, Michigan: Michigan Grill Dinner, 214–218; Rhubarb Mousse in Cookie Tulip, 202

Odessa Piper (owner); Eric Rupert (co-chef), L'Etoile Restaurant, Madison, Wisconsin: Great Lakes Whitefish with Basil Cream Sauce and Golden Whitefish Roe, 101

Patricia J. Pooley, The Moveable Feast Restaurant, Ann Arbor, Michigan: Carthusian Grilled Salmon, 108

David Radwine, Springfield, Illinois: Cappuccino Cookies, 182

BARBARA GRUNES

For several years a food columnist and restaurant critic for the *Chicago Sun Times*, Barbara Grunes is enjoying her current calling as best-selling author of more than three dozen cookbooks.

Barbara's concern for the meticulous recording of traditional regional specialties is not lessened by her interest in innovative cuisine, as she so ably demonstrates in the *Heartland Food Society Cookbook*. As a mother of five, Barbara has had plenty of experience in combining the art of cooking with the practicality of pleasing a diverse group of tastes.

The *Heartland Food Society Cookbook* is only the newest of her authoritative cookbooks. Her modern standards include *Skinny Pizza*, *Kabobs on the Grill*, *Skinny Chocolate*, and the highly-regarded *Fish on the Grill*, which has sold more than 450,000 copies. With more than thirty titles to her credit, Barbara Grunes is redefining "good taste."